Mapping Managerial
Implications of
Green Strategy

A Framework for Sustainable Innovation

Mapping Managerial Implications of
Green Strategy

A Framework for Sustainable Innovation

George Tesar
Umeå University, Sweden & University of Wisconsin-Whitewater, USA

Hamid Moini
University of Wisconsin-Whitewater, USA

Olav Jull Sørensen
Aalborg University, Denmark

NEW JERSEY · LONDON · SINGAPORE · BEIJING · SHANGHAI · HONG KONG · TAIPEI · CHENNAI · TOKYO

Published by

World Scientific Publishing Europe Ltd.

57 Shelton Street, Covent Garden, London WC2H 9HE

Head office: 5 Toh Tuck Link, Singapore 596224

USA office: 27 Warren Street, Suite 401-402, Hackensack, NJ 07601

Library of Congress Cataloging-in-Publication Data

Names: Tesar, George, author. | Moini, Hamid, author. | Sørensen, Olav Jull, author.
Title: Mapping managerial implications of green strategy : a framework for sustainable innovation /
    by George Tesar (Umeå University, Sweden & University of Wisconsin-Whitewater, USA),
    Hamid Moini (University of Wisconsin-Whitewater, USA),
    Olav Jull Sørensen (Aalborg University, Denmark).
Description: New Jersey : World Scientific, [2018] | Includes bibliographical references and index.
Identifiers: LCCN 2017051222 | ISBN 9781786344809 (hc : alk. paper)
Subjects: LCSH: Green marketing. | Management--Environmental aspects. |
    Sustainable development.
Classification: LCC HF5413 .T43 2018 | DDC 658.4/08--dc23
LC record available at https://lccn.loc.gov/2017051222

British Library Cataloguing-in-Publication Data
A catalogue record for this book is available from the British Library.

For any available supplementary material, please visit
http://www.worldscientific.com/worldscibooks/10.1142/Q0140#t=suppl

Desk Editors: Suraj Kumar/Jennifer Brough/Koe Shi Ying

Typeset by Stallion Press
Email: enquiries@stallionpress.com

Printed in Singapore

This book is dedicated to

My Sluníčko
Mitra and Sheila

Preface

This book is the product of an international effort by academics interested in how managers of smaller manufacturing enterprises face the challenges of becoming green. For academics, becoming green is an emerging worldwide trend driven by consumers and legislative actions of national governments. Academics believe that it can be easily defined and researched. For managers of smaller manufacturing enterprises, becoming green is difficult to understand and address, and requires commitment.

Commitment to green marketing initiatives by managers of smaller manufacturing enterprises varies enormously throughout the world. Danish managers believe that Denmark has the highest number of smaller green manufacturing enterprises. But not all countries are like Denmark. Some countries have difficulties convincing the public, including consumers and managers, that environmental concerns are real. Politically unstable countries, countries that are economically and socially challenged, focus on issues other than depletion of nonrenewable resources, air pollution, or shortages of clean drinking water, to mention just a few green concerns. Nevertheless, managers of smaller manufacturing enterprises today, wherever they are in the world, face emerging green initiatives.

This book is for managers of smaller manufacturing enterprises who face green challenges and find it frustrating to make a commitment to green initiatives. This book is not a handbook in the traditional sense, but is intended to provide these managers with a framework for analysis and introspection. Not all managers are willing to make a commitment to green initiatives, but for those willing do so by developing and marketing green products and services, we provide an approach based in the philosophy of modern marketing management. The content of this book is based on the authors' many experiences working with international projects as academics, researchers, and consultants. Our visits with colleagues in different countries frequently led to productive discussions of so called green managerial challenges. The authors present tools and approaches designed to help managers of smaller manufacturing enterprises confront present and future green challenges.

We have observed how green challenges impact the public in different countries during our international experiences. Responses to the "green" challenge are seen in Sweden, Finland, and Denmark where older buildings in many cities are refurbished to be energy efficient and coastal areas are planted with wind turbines. At Aalborg University in Aalborg, Denmark where the study that is the basis for this book originated, old industrial structures are reconfigured into fashionable apartment and office buildings. In Sweden, garbage is used to generate steam power and heat the entire region around the town of Umeå; in winter the town center is free of snow and ice because its walkways are heated. There, energy generation is so profitable that garbage is imported from neighboring Norway. However, Nordic style recycling is still on the horizon in the Czech Republic and Slovakia. We wanted to find out why these differences exist.

Managers of smaller manufacturing enterprises face green challenges directly and indirectly: directly, due to legislative actions, increased demand for green products and services, or competitive pressures; indirectly, by pressure from environmental trends, operating in changing industrial structures, or hearing from green consumers dissatisfied with traditional energy consuming products or services. Consumers are demanding green products and services from smaller manufacturing enterprises since, in many countries, they represent the overwhelming majority of producers of consumer products and services. Some smaller manufacturing enterprises commit their resources and managerial skills to green products and services, but others do not.

Many colleagues have contributed directly or indirectly to this book. The VELUX Group and the International Business Centre at Aalborg University made it possible to conduct a major study of Danish managers concerning responses to green challenges. We talked with managers of smaller manufacturing enterprises in Europe and North America. These discussions gave us opportunities to verify some of our research findings. The managers with whom we talked agreed that demand for green products and services came directly from consumers. In markets where green consumers are active and their voices are heard, demand for green products and services is high. In some countries, the government mandates green products and services in various industries. Yet, managers of smaller manufacturing enterprises globally are reluctant to respond to either.

We believe this book should help managers of smaller manufacturing enterprises understand the many aspects of becoming green and help them formulate profitable and competitive green marketing strategies. We thank everyone involved for their constructive inputs.

George Tesar
Madison, Wisconsin

Hamid Moini
Madison, Wisconsin

Olav Jull Sørensen
Aalborg, Denmark

About the Authors

 **George Tesar** is a Professor Emeritus of Marketing and International Business at Umeå University in Umeå, Sweden and Professor Emeritus at the University of Wisconsin–Whitewater. He is an Adjunct Professor at Aalborg University in Denmark. Professor Tesar is a coauthor of several books on applications of marketing and recently coauthored a book on innovative applications of marketing management in the African context. Professor Tesar has a doctorate from the University of Wisconsin–Madison and an MBA from Michigan State University. He is a mechanical engineer with several years of industry experience. He has served on several boards and is professionally active as a consultant training academics, executives, and managers in technology transfer, internationalization, and foreign market entry strategies. He is a founding member of the Product Development and Management Association, a professional association focusing on technology transfer and new product development. He is active in international student and faculty exchanges and a member of the Fulbright Association. Professor Tesar lectures abroad extensively, and can be reached at tesarg@uww.edu.

Hamid Moini is an Emeritus Professor of Finance at University of Wisconsin–Whitewater. Professor Moini received his Ph.D. in Financial Economics and Master of Art in Finance from the University of Alabama. Over the past 30 years, he has focused on development of global market entry strategies for smaller firms, international mergers and acquisitions, and management education in the contemporary global context. He has published two books and numerous refereed articles in the leading journals in finance and international business. Because of his extensive interest in internationalization of small- and medium-sized enterprises, he has been invited to several international networks, study groups, and a number of European universities to give lectures and seminars. In his consulting practice, Dr. Moini offers a range of services including planning for foreign direct investments, capital budgeting, and financial structure along with cross-cultural training for managers. He works closely with top management through workshops, seminars, and on-going internal assessment programs. Professor Moini can be reached at moinia@uww.edu.

O. Jull Sørensen has been a Professor of International Business at Aalborg University since 1991 and Head of the International Business Centre (IBC) since its establishment in 1984. Today, the Centre hosts three graduate educational programs within the field of International Business; a Ph.D. program, and a core team of 14 researchers of 14. His main research interests are (1) Internationalization of companies, (2) International industrial dynamics and value chain analysis, and (3) Government–Business relations. The topics are being researched in a developed market perspective as well as a developing/transition country perspective. He has been a lead scholar in research, capacity building, and educational projects in Africa (Ghana, Tanzania);

Eastern Europe (Lithuania) and Russia, and Asia (Vietnam and China). He is a member of the Academic Council for Social Sciences, Aalborg University and the Council of the Department of Business and Management. He is also a council member of Nordic Centre at Fudan University, China, and since 2010, he has been the director of the Sino-Danish Center (SDC)-Innovation Management program in China comprising a graduate program, a research program, as well as collaboration with the business community in China. Professor Sørensen can be reached at ojs@business.aau.dk.

Contents

Recommended Readings   108

**Chapter 6.   Competitive Positioning Subject
             to Green Marketing Strategies   111**

6.1   Specification of a Competitive Position   113

     6.1.1   Geographic competitive relationships   115

     6.1.2   Marketing competitive relationships   117

     6.1.3   Market position and competitive advantage . . .   120

     6.1.4   External analysis   123

6.2   Competitive Positions and Technological

     Capabilities   124

     6.2.1   Consumer motivations   125

Recommended Reading   127

**Chapter 7.   Emerging Green Concerns
             and Managers of Smaller
             Manufacturing Enterprises   129**

7.1   Market Responses by Smaller Manufacturing

     Enterprises   131

7.2   Consumer Responses to Green Products and

     Services   133

7.3   Consumption Experiences of Green Consumers   136

7.4   Consumption Patterns of Green Consumers   138

7.5   Post-Consumption and Product and Service

     Residuals   142

Recommended Reading   143

**Chapter 8.   International Implications of Green
             Strategies and Consumption Behavior   145**

8.1   International Markets and Technology   146

     8.1.1   Cultural conditions   148

     8.1.2   Resources   148

     8.1.3   Awareness   150

Chapter 1

Introduction to Managerial Implications of Green Strategy

In one of our recent studies in Denmark, a manager of a smaller manufacturing enterprise told us that governments do not motivate managers to be green consumers. Consumers are concerned about conservation of natural resources, sustainability, and green products and services. Managers respond to consumers' demands because they remain profitable if they do so. We received similar responses from other Danish managers later in the study. Danish managers are not unique; managers of smaller manufacturing enterprises in North America, Europe, and other parts of the world share similar opinions. In the minds of consumers worldwide, green products and services are important to them and their consumption; they closely link consumption of green products and services with their lifestyles and their own overall well-being as well as of their families.

Smaller manufacturing enterprises are the engines of economic development and growth. They are sources of new ideas, innovation, and creative technologies. From an economic perspective, small manufacturing enterprises create jobs, increase tax revenues, and stabilize economic development and growth. From a social perspective, they stabilize communities and geographic regions by increasing income, reducing social unrest, and improving quality of life.

Many rural geographic regions, both larger and smaller cities, and localities that have lost manufacturing opportunities are founding incubators for entrepreneurs to start new ventures; establishing research and development parks by converting existing structures or building new facilities; or offering favorable locations as manufacturing sites on publicly supported industrial grounds. These attempts are motivated by studies and experiences indicating that smaller manufacturing enterprises are important and necessary cornerstones of technological development and competitive growth.

From the perspectives of economic and regional development, smaller manufacturing enterprises are encouraged to form industrial clusters by cooperating with their suppliers, customers, and, in some cases, competitors, to innovate, improve their marketing activities, or form value chains that can reach customers in new markets around the world. Smaller manufacturing enterprises become more competitive and innovative, and grow into large enterprises that compete in the global market place on more dynamic levels when strengthening ties.

It is important to note that not all smaller manufacturing enterprises operate at the technological and competitive cutting edge. Some are very much product or process oriented and have limited competitive exposure in the market. For example, some smaller manufacturing enterprises provide fabrication services for established clients who are aware of their reputation for quality and service. Other smaller manufacturing enterprises become active in markets where, because of their entrepreneurial propensities, they offer innovative products and services. Such smaller manufacturing enterprises incorporate new technologies, identify new consumption trends, or respond quickly to changes in regulatory edicts. Smaller manufacturing enterprises managed by more experienced rational managers operate in well-defined markets, in segments that are homogeneous and easily serviceable, and offer products or services that meet the needs of their clients, customers, consumers, or users. To various degrees, all three types of smaller manufacturing enterprises need to accept challenges, face problems, and introduce changes in their marketing initiatives. The major dilemma is to identify smaller manufacturing enterprises that are willing to accept the challenges proactively and those that are motivated by last minute regulatory actions, competitive pressures, or loss of market share.

Conservation of natural resources, sustainability, and market or socially motivated green strategies present challenges that are perceived by managers as dilemmas, strategic and operational problems, or even major survival threats to the entire entity. Managers of smaller manufacturing enterprises perceive green strategy on several levels. Green strategy, frequently driven by various interest groups and emerging from concern for the physical environment as communicated via the public media, is perhaps the most common. Green strategy also emanates from markets where interest groups or consumer movements are most active. The latter are generally associated with products or services that have greater market visibility or presence such as automotive products, products with chemical content, or services that require vast energy use. However, it is the third type of green strategy that generates significant concerns among managers of smaller manufacturing enterprises, and green strategy has a direct impact on their own products and services: when their consumers ask for substitution of materials, parts and components to be made from renewable materials, product ingredients that do not harm their health or lifestyles, in addition to many other demands from current consumers.

Whether managers of smaller manufacturing enterprises choose to be proactive or wait until ultimate pressures force them to react, they should develop their own green strategy very much embedded in marketing activities. For managers of smaller manufacturing enterprises, the green strategy broadly defined by the market place needs to be transformed into strategically based green marketing strategies.

In order to meet the challenges of renewable resources, sustainability, and green strategy in the future, managers of smaller manufacturing enterprises will have to assess their technological capabilities in addition to formulating marketing strategies more creatively in order to maintain a steady pace with the ever-increasing sophistication of green products and services entering the market place. Consumption and post-consumption behavior of their consumers will determine the nature and urgency of their green marketing strategies.

Our objective is to assist managers of smaller manufacturing enterprises with their own mapping of the managerial challenges and implications of green strategy. This is a complex and unwieldy task due to the variety of smaller manufacturing enterprises. Nevertheless, the contribution of this presentation is a comprehensive conceptual framework designed to help managers understand the factors within their managerial span of control that are directly influenced by issues of renewable resources, sustainability, and green strategy that lead directly to formulation of green marketing strategies. We trust that this effort will lead to green philosophies and practices that in turn will create new innovative, competitive, and profitable green marketing strategies.

1.1   Markets and Green Strategy

In more-advanced markets where conservation, sustainability, and green products and services are socially and economically visible, consumers are more likely to commit to green consumption options followed by practical post-consumption behavior. In advanced markets, marketing managers are asked to market products that do not diminish natural resources. Consumers want products that can be easily recycled at the end of their life cycles. They ask for packaging made from recycled material, they lower the cost of electricity by wearing clothing that does not wrinkle, or save energy by using public transportation. Consumers do not want to tamper with ecological balances; instead, as much as possible, they want to reduce their own carbon footprints. Consumers' attempts to reduce their carbon footprints present a dilemma for marketing managers who must change the way products are produced; they must reduce the use of chemicals, substitute materials, or reduce their own energy consumption. These are only a few examples of how managers of manufacturing enterprises of all sizes need to confront rapidly changing and internationally competitive consumer and business-to-business markets.

In the competitive world of global marketing, managers need to be constantly aware of developments around them. The growing emphases on sustainability of nonrenewable resources combined with changes in consumers' consumption and post-consumption behaviors are major forces that eventually define how managers allocate their resources, market products and services, and compete. Most managers regard sustainability as an evolving force that is inevitably changing how they formulate their marketing strategies. More proactive managers believe that sustainability requires innovative approaches that will lead to closer cooperation among all stakeholders — ranging from socially, economically, and politically driven environmental activists to average consumers dedicated to innovative green consumption and post-consumption behavior.

The above approach, advocated by more proactive managers, requires new perspectives on how managers relate to widespread societal challenges. These challenges are deeply rooted in global environments. Managers must consider how they formulate innovative green marketing strategies and communicate their efforts to consumers. The new behavioral perspectives regarding ecologically motivated consumers necessitate comprehensive examination of entire value chains as the first step in developing a framework essential to guiding sustainable innovations embedded in green marketing strategies in consumer-driven consumption and post-consumption processes.

Managers of smaller manufacturing enterprises face ever-greater environmental challenges — major societal transformations that demand reactions to not only markets and customers, but also to public policies, regulations, laws, and social movements. Most managers of smaller manufacturing enterprises generally consider such challenges as important inputs into their decisions, while some are reluctant to recognize these developments. Nevertheless, they must respond to them in the future if they want to retain their markets, compete, and be profitable.

Most managers of smaller manufacturing enterprises believe that challenges of conservation, sustainability, and green strategy may be offset by innovation. By introducing new ideas, inventions, or new ways of performing operations and tasks, managers can solve many of these challenges. In the process of dealing with these challenges, managers must strive to apply new knowledge, introduce innovative technology, and create new solutions, among other activities. New green products and services require new technologies. For example, coal powered plants generating electricity are made technologically obsolete by solar or wind power installations just as much as hybrid and purely electric propulsion systems replace conventional internal combustion engines in automobiles.

Conservation, sustainability, and green strategy today are proxies for a range of ecologically related actions that evolve into managerial challenges which directly impact market dynamics, consumption and post-consumption issues, and the ability to compete. In a fluid social context, conservation, sustainability, and green strategy are perceived as attempts not to harm the physical environment in which managers make their decisions, and at the same time, not to deplete the natural resources needed to develop and market products and services entering the marketplace. Managers are asked to make every effort to achieve long-term ecological balance. For many managers of smaller manufacturing enterprises, the solutions to these challenges depend on their ability to make innovative decisions and the richness of the resources they manage.

Large international enterprises, with adequate resources, generally perceive sustainability challenges as broad, and sometimes elusive, societal trends that need to be addressed with financial and marketing restraint across markets. When appropriate, large international enterprises search for innovative approaches on all levels of marketing initiatives to satisfy specific markets where conservation, sustainability, and green strategy are issues. They tend to service markets where market sensitivity to these issues differs significantly. Their managerial philosophy on these issues is frequently more flexible toward individual markets. Smaller manufacturing enterprises typically do not have abundant resources and must be even more flexible in their formulation of marketing strategies to confront similar challenges of conservation, sustainability, and green strategy.

Managers of smaller manufacturing enterprises face additional challenges. They are less internationally motivated. In their domestic markets, they view green strategy more pragmatically. If, or when, they attempt to understand the fundamental relationships between their marketing practices and the overall ecological issues that have bearings on their decisions, they often wait until they receive market or competitive signals. Some smaller manufacturing enterprises also market their products and services in the global marketplace. If they do, they need to understand the substantial importance of green strategy. In order to formulate competitive green marketing strategies, they need information about their consumers, markets, and competitors and what perceptions, attitudes, and preferences they have toward green marketing strategies. Managers of smaller manufacturing enterprises need such information to decide what approaches will be critical for them to progress toward a sustainable future and continue managing in globally competitive markets.

1.2 Managerial Challenges

Managers are responsible for constantly tracking and assessing changes around them that impact their decisions. Many changes, especially those in their immediate environment and relevant to their strategic decision making, typically turn into challenges. For example, rapid technological changes that drive new products into markets also introduce new materials, manufacturing procedures, and steep learning curves. The new materials and manufacturing procedures may also contribute to pollution and ecological hazards. Equally so, technological changes may contribute to new lifestyles. Lifestyles in turn change consumers' behavior and consumption patterns as demonstrated, among other things, by the Internet. Changing lifestyles have a direct bearing on society. Lifestyles and consumption can change social norms and expectations. The combination of new social values, changing consumption behavior, and new technology has compelling economic consequences. Managers of smaller manufacturing enterprises need to consider all of these dimensions in their decisions.

In marketing-oriented enterprises, the formulation of market-ing strategies is typically influenced by challenges that managers can identify as directly related to their markets, consumers, and even their competitors. Managers of smaller manufacturing enter-prises perceive, define, and specify ecological challenges in their relevant environments as having direct impact on formulation of green marketing strategies. Among these managers, green marketing strategies are market necessities. They realize that formulations of green marketing strategies require close coordination of several functions such as marketing, finance, and manufacturing, among others. However, not all managers relate conservation, sustainability, and green strategy challenges directly to their own marketing strategies. They tend to arrange these challenges according to the available resources and the time needed to resolve them. Some conservation, sustainability, and green strategy challenges may guide future development of green marketing strategies and more lasting innovation. These are difficult decisions for most managers of smaller manufacturing enterprises.

It is difficult for managers of smaller manufacturing enterprises to respond to the above challenges leading to green marketing strategies. They must cooperate with a variety of stakeholders with differing opinions concerning conservation, sustainability, and/or green strategy. They recognize that their principal stakeholders are customers, consumers, and users of their own products and services who respond to their own social and economic needs. Other stakeholders are owners, investors, bankers, and venture capitalists among others. Due to the nature of global markets today, important stakeholders also include domestic or international regulatory agen-cies, nongovernmental organizations, and other interest groups. The combination of challenges initiated by various stakeholders regarding these issues may, in the future, completely change the market and competitive dynamics of smaller manufacturing enterprises.

Increasing demands from some stakeholders to accept green challenges imply significant financial commitments and reassessment of financial resources. More specifically, changing cost dynamics have a direct bearing on the formulation of green marketing strategies since they require analyses of resources and existing infrastructures. Will the existing infrastructure facilitate the additional requirements of green innovation marketing strategies? Some managers of smaller manufacturing enterprises consider changing cost dynamics and any resulting financial commitments comparable to decisions leading to new market development, diversification, or acquisition.

From the marketing and financial management perspectives of less internationally active, smaller manufacturing enterprises, the lack of understanding of international standards can make the formation of international marketing strategies overwhelming. Their managers are often dependent on unsubstantiated information from dubious sources. This is frequently evident among smaller manufacturing enterprises that provide fabrication services or manufacture products in limited numbers for foreign clients. These types of services require close contact with clients and are subject to contractual specifications. Under these conditions, ecological standards and notions of conservation, sustainability, or green strategy among international markets may vary significantly and need to be negotiated. A similar situation exists among exporters of a variety of consumer products designated specifically for export.

1.3 Path to Green Innovation

Innovative managers of smaller manufacturing enterprises realize that the path to conservation, sustainability, and green strategy requires information. This need for increased data and information management means changes in how data and information are gathered internally and externally. Data and information need to be processed and distributed directly to decision makers. Expansion of information management among smaller manufacturing enterprises tends to foster greater reliance on marketing management and a more integrated multifunctional approach to management in general.

The challenges emerging from perceptions and interpretations of conventional conservation, sustainability, and green strategy among managers of smaller manufacturing enterprises initially present an assortment of strategic and operational problems. The most important challenges start with potentially positively or, in some instances, negatively perceived characteristics of green strategy. Managers usually advance through a sequential process of rationalization and adoption before they decide to formulate green marketing strategies. As managers begin to formulate and implement green marketing strategies, they modify their perceptions and interpretations. For more innovative smaller manufacturing enterprises, green marketing strategies become integral parts of their overall marketing activities.

For smaller manufacturing enterprises the distinct, and sometimes singular, events involving formulation of green marketing strategies often require innovative organizational approaches. These include systematic and objective review of the mission, reappraisal of the entire value chain, and in-depth review of both consumption and post-consumption behaviors of their consumers. Depending on the marketing approaches used by managers of smaller manufacturing enterprises and their technological sophistication, there might be other factors that need close examination before successful green marketing strategies can be formulated.

From a marketing point of view, the information gathered from reexamining internal and external managerial perspectives can also generate new knowledge for managers of smaller manufacturing enterprises. Such newly acquired knowledge often leads to new philosophies and innovative approaches of doing things. For most managers of smaller manufacturing enterprises this shift in thinking and decision making leads to a new mindset. In contemporary marketing management, new mindsets are the necessary prerequisites to construction of green marketing strategies.

Among marketing-oriented managers of smaller manufacturing enterprises, green marketing strategies presume that all managers understand and accept the relevant aspects of conservation, sustainability, and green strategy. This implies that managers make appropriate decisions to internalize these notions as integral parts of their managerial thinking and, consequently, introduce appropriate innovative guidelines to shape formulation of green marketing strategies. These are the assumptions on which this presentation is based. Conceptualization and construction of a comprehensive green framework unique to each enterprise are required in developing guidelines by which green decisions are made and implemented in green marketing strategies.

Because managers of smaller manufacturing enterprises usually have a more day-to-day approach to management, they need more practical ways to address relevant issues of green marketing strategies. As suggested above, this requires innovative approaches to organizational development and management — most likely a combination of marketing, financial, and engineering specialists familiar with green issues. Simultaneously, green issues require comprehensive understanding of market demand. Because markets are constantly changing, managers of smaller manufacturing enterprises are dependent on a constant flow of information from both domestic and international markets and need to understand their dimensions.

1.4   Markets

Market dimensions and operational parameters are set by domestic authorities and differ from country to country. They typically include policies concerning energy sources and utilization, financial oversight, administration of energy uses, and energy sustainability concerns. In general, these are combined with future expectation and eventual development of alternative energy sources. In most domestic markets, primary considerations related to green strategy are questions of energy generation and utilization. Consumer behavior, consumption levels, or post-consumption concerns are not generally included. Ecological aspects are normally left to the prevalent market mechanism.

International dimensions of markets consist mostly of attempts to utilize and conserve natural resources. This fundamental concern typically directs production of raw material and may attempt to influence its consumption. Many international entities strive to conserve natural resources and find suitable alternatives for nonrenewable resources. Secondary concerns address formation of smaller innovative enterprises expecting that such enterprises will more likely find energy alternatives and substitution options for nonrenewable resources. However, many of these initiatives require government assistance and are generally undercapitalized. Government agencies occasionally attempt to stimulate development of new energy sources directly by establishing programs to internally identify innovative ways to sustain availability of natural resources. These programs require innovative approaches that may not be internally available in economically challenged countries.

The level of internationalization among smaller manufacturing enterprises and their acceptance and commitment to green marketing strategies appear to be closely linked with the types of markets they serve. Consumers have more influence on product offerings in more economically and technologically developed markets. Managers operating in more developed markets stress green marketing strategies more than in less-advanced markets where consumer inputs tend to be minimal. In many international markets, implementation of green marketing strategies is closely connected with commonly accepted levels of technology.

High technology-focused markets tend to be more product and service sensitive and concerned with energy utilization, conservation of natural resources, and sustainability in general, and are more likely to demand greater attention to availability of green products and services. In some markets, consumers frequently articulate green concerns as part of their consumption and post-consumption preferences. In less technologically feasible markets, consumers require a longer acceptance time for green products and services.

Concerns over green consumption and post-consumption start with recognition and acceptance of public ecological concerns by consumers in both domestic and international markets. Consumers' recognition of relationships between the overall physical environment and their individual consumption drives formulation and implementation by domestic or international marketers of many green marketing strategies. Interventions by government agencies often enter only after marketing managers resist or challenge demands of consumers.

Governmental agencies in many countries take the initiative to stimulate formation of green marketing strategies among smaller manufacturing enterprises. However, the results have been marginal and additional incentives received directly from markets are needed. Managers of smaller manufacturing enterprises particularly feel that government incentives, and occasionally even market incentives, may result in lower profitability. In order to remain profitable, they need to reexamine their value creation processes and adjust them to meet the expectations of regulatory and market actions. This requires reexamination, and eventual reconfiguration, of not only marketing initiatives, but also implies systematic rethinking of overall strategic objectives.

1.5   Green Challenges

Smaller manufacturing enterprises around the world are challenged daily by green initiatives. Many green initiatives come directly from consumers, while others are imposed by regulatory agencies, special interest groups, or nongovernmental organizations. Government agencies in some countries present both directives and incentives for enterprises of all sizes to introduce innovative green marketing strategies. Mangers of smaller manufacturing enterprises often do not take advantage of government incentives. When confronted with rapidly emerging green issues, most of them have little experience in integrating green innovative options in their marketing activities. They often lack understanding of how green challenges may change their decisions, reallocate their resources, and refocus their marketing initiatives.

Managers of smaller manufacturing enterprises frequently suggest that they do not have the necessary financial resources to even consider including green concerns in their marketing activities — green concerns cut into profits. They also point out that there is a sizable shortage of financial, marketing, and engineering specialists familiar with green issues who can assess the importance of green issues within the context of proprietary green marketing strategies. According to many managers of smaller manufacturing enterprises, green issues are public issues. These managers do not understand how green technological consequences connected with green issues will interact with their markets in the future.

Most managers of smaller manufacturing enterprises do not anticipate that any changes in their marketing strategies due to green issues will change patterns of consumption. However, if changes in patterns of consumption do materialize, they will also modify consumers' post-consumption behavior — which will present new challenges. Current market trends clearly indicate that, in the future, consumers will insist manufacturers be required to recycle, otherwise eliminate, or dispose of any residuals of consumption. Such outcomes will further increase marketing costs.

It is difficult for managers of smaller manufacturing enterprises to understand the fundamental relationships between their marketing practices and the overall physical and social environments around them. They need to understand, in light of changing ecological dynamics, how consumers will behave in the global market place in the future. Consumers will decide on what consumption and post-consumption approaches they will take toward a sustainable future. Managers of smaller manufacturing enterprises must formulate their green marketing strategies creatively to respond to consumers' notions of sustainability.

Green markets are rapidly evolving and need innovative green marketing strategies. For smaller manufacturing enterprises to remain competitive in rapidly changing green markets, they must become more proactive — broaden their missions, reassess their resource allocations, expand their managerial diversity, and include managers who specialize in green challenges. At the same time, they must forge closer ties with green consumers. These are major changes in how smaller manufacturing enterprises must approach their goals, reach markets, and maintain profitability. For many managers of smaller manufacturing enterprises, these changes may require complete restructuring, new strategic and operational modes, and new perspectives on green initiatives, in other words, a new strategic framework for management.

1.6   Mapping Managerial Implications

This book is intended for managers of smaller manufacturing enterprises who are responsible for strategic and operational decisions concerning green issues. More specifically, they are responsible for issues directly related to such contemporary managerial challenges and considerations as conservation, sustainability, more effective and efficient utilization of natural resources, development of renewable resources, energy generation, and achievement of smaller carbon footprints, among other issues related to green marketing strategies. Many of these issues are consumer driven, or user driven in business-to-business marketing. Most managers of smaller manufacturing enterprises today perceive formulation and implementation of green marketing strategies, and subsequent marketing operations, as competitively necessary in global markets.

A more tangible objective is the introduction of a new strategic framework, uniquely suited for marketing managers of smaller manufacturing enterprises, to guide them in formulation and implementation of green marketing strategies. An enterprise needs to map out all relevant aspects of its managerial philosophies and practices in order to develop its own unique green framework. Within such a framework, a smaller manufacturing enterprise will be able to scan and assess environmental stimuli which often act as constraints on their propensity to make decisions concerning green initiatives. Formulation of a new green strategic framework is a formidable task for most managers of smaller manufacturing enterprises.

The proposed strategic framework integrates several interrelated components to provide a better understanding of how green marketing strategies may be conceptualized and formulated within the unique philosophy and operation of a given enterprise. The major components of the framework are: (1) environmental forces external to an enterprise, (2) enterprise initiatives based on its philosophy of marketing management, (3) approaches to formulation of green marketing and financial strategies, and (4) dimensions of competitive positioning of green marketing strategies. These components are combined with considerations of emerging societal and market concerns dealing with green marketing strategies, including consumption and post-consumption trends, and finally, consideration of components dealing with international dimensions.

Recommended Readings

1. Berger, S. (2013). *Making in America*: *From Innovation to Market* (The MIT Press, Cambridge, MA).
2. Drucker, P. F. (1964). *Managing for Results* (Harper & Row, Publishers, New York, NY).
3. Tesar, G. and Bodin, J. (2013). *Marketing Management in Geographically Remote Industrial Clusters*: *Implications for Business-to-Customer Marketing* (World Scientific Publishing Company, Singapore).
4. Tesar, G., Moini, H., Kuada, J. and Sørensen, O. J. (2010). *Smaller Manufacturing Enterprises in an International Context: A Longitudinal Exploration* (Imperial College Press, London, UK).

Chapter 2

Commitment to Green Strategy and External Forces

Smaller manufacturing enterprises do not exist in a vacuum. They operate in environments that produce a variety of positive and negative forces that shape their missions; impact levels of resources; influence competitive market positions; and most of all, define relationships with markets and consumers. Environmental forces also set societal limits within which smaller manufacturing enterprises respond to consumers' demands, market their products and services, and compete. The major problem faced by managers of smaller manufacturing enterprises is the reality that these forces are turbulent and change rapidly. Managers must understand that environmental forces, directly and indirectly, influence the strategic and operational management of enterprises and their marketing initiatives. Directly by setting limits and guidelines within which market related decisions are made, and indirectly by understanding how marketing initiatives fit into broad, dynamic, and interrelated societal structures around them. Consequently, managers of smaller manufacturing enterprises must consider how environmental forces influence their strategic and operational decisions.

Environmental forces can be immense and represent an overwhelming burden of constraints, especially for managers of less dynamic smaller manufacturing enterprises. Environmental forces range from broad technological innovations and developments, changing macro- and micro-economic conditions, unpredictable and fluctuating behavior of consumers, elusive lifestyles, and growing social pressures resulting in government regulations. Managers must decide to what extent environmental forces facilitate or impede their marketing activities. These are complex decisions that managers must make considering their generally limited resources. Environmental forces have a direct bearing on the future and ultimately survival of some smaller manufacturing enterprises depending on their profitability.

Conservation, sustainability, and green strategy are the growing dominant forces in the immediate environment that present major challenges for managers of smaller manufacturing enterprises. Conservation and sustainability are the most critical challenges; green strategy is a proxy for both. Managers must decide how relevant these forces are to their marketing initiatives and to what extent they are willing to commit resources to reduce or eliminate them. Society, and most importantly consumers, perceive conservation and sustainability as the most important forces for managers of smaller manufacturing enterprises to address. However, the most important force is green strategy. For most smaller manufacturing enterprises, the decision to respond to green strategy requires fundamentally reformulating their marketing strategies and future marketing initiatives.

2.1   Green Strategy Challenge

Although conservation and sustainability are relevant issues for managers of smaller manufacturing enterprises, green strategy is the most relevant. Green strategy is an ambiguous social concept. In broad managerial terms, green strategy is defined as a process concerned with rational utilization of societal and enterprise resources, energy particularly. Societal expectations also include reduction in consumption of natural resources and development of alternatives for nonrenewable resources. The notion of green strategy embodies these fundamental concepts. However, for managers of smaller manufacturing enterprises, the societal definition of green strategy is a broad operational concept. Managers need to interpret this definition of green strategy and find a direct connection to their own green philosophy and conceptualize a level of commitment to it.

Green strategy provides the general framework constructed by society and partially redefined by consumers as guidelines that shape demand for green consumer products and services. When consuming products and/or using services, consumers set their preferences to meet, or exceed, their expectations of what green products or services represent in their consumption preferences. From another perspective, consumers interpret the broad societal notion of green strategy and attempt to place their interpretation of green strategy in the context of their psychological, social, or economic consumption experiences. These experiences are then communicated directly or indirectly, and most often through social media, to decision makers of smaller manufacturing enterprises who are expected to respond by modifying existing products or services, or developing new ones to meet consumer expectations of green products and services.

Managers of smaller manufacturing enterprises frequently reduce the broad notion of green strategy to a more manageable green marketing, and more specifically, green marketing strategies. This effort requires each enterprise to redefine its mission and conduct a systematic assessment of its resource base. These two activities determine the extent of how green initiatives, including consumers' expectations, will be integrated into all future marketing initiatives. Some smaller manufacturing enterprises are able to internalize green activities more easily than others. Also, some are more skillful and innovative communicating with consumers about green issues. Open communication with consumers and the public is one of the cornerstones of implementing notions of green strategy.

The greatest challenges posed by green strategy for smaller manufacturing enterprises are the multifaceted and unique interpretations by managers. Depending on their managerial philosophies, managers must grasp what green strategy represents in society and how it directly influences their marketing initiatives. More specifically, managers' understanding of how green strategy directly influences formulation of green marketing strategies often leads to new green philosophies in individual enterprises. Acceptance of a green strategy indicates how extensively a smaller manufacturing enterprise is committed to its new green philosophy and eventual green marketing strategies. Different levels of commitment to green marketing strategies are to be expected because of the strategic diversity among smaller manufacturing enterprises.

2.2   External Forces

Many external forces influence changes among smaller manufacturing enterprises. Depending on the level of managerial and strategic orientation, managers must identify the forces that are most relevant to their success and survival. Important external forces for smaller manufacturing enterprises involve: (1) technological, (2) economic, (3) social, and (4) lifestyle forces. Technological forces help determine the level at which an enterprise is willing to function and directly control the functional, physical, and psychological makeup of products or services. Economic forces drive both the strategic enterprise level by motivating its market success and the operational level by guiding allocation of controllable resources. Social forces consist of ethical, political, and legal constraints within which enterprises define their missions and formulate their strategies. Finally, lifestyle forces create the social and personal needs, wants, and preferences that formulate markets.

2.2.1   *Technological forces*

Smaller manufacturing enterprises differ substantially on the scale of technological sophistication. Some begin as high technology enterprises, frequently managed by individuals with scientific, technical, or managerial expertise, and improve their technological capabilities even further as they grow. Others begin as low technology enterprises managed by craftsmen or technicians and perform simple tasks or are generally single product or service operations.

Some smaller manufacturing enterprises tend to have relatively long life spans, while others do not survive past their first year of existence. If low technology enterprises survive, they are met with several options. They can respond to changing technological forces around them and grow into high technology enterprises or continue the *status quo*. Technological sophistication of individual enterprises is mostly an internal decision. Each enterprise determines its own technological preferences and limits. Managers make such decisions based on their preferences for markets, market segments, and consumers. The technological sophistication of consumers may determine the technological sophistication of an enterprise.

Depending on how technology relevant to their strategies and operations evolves, technological forces have differing impacts on smaller manufacturing enterprises. Technology may be continuous, evolving at various rates along its technological path, and steadily increase the technological capabilities of an enterprise. An enterprise may consider its technological path at any point in time and decide how appropriate the technology is for its markets and consumers. When technology is continuous, it is also predictable. Enterprises can plan and modify their technological capabilities and expected growth accordingly. They can improve their products and services and inform consumers about pending technological improvements. Enterprises that choose not to improve their technological sophistication, for whatever reason, may simply service their markets with existing products or services and expect them to eventually become obsolete. Smaller manufacturing enterprises may shift to markets where technologically lower products and services are in demand if their products or services, in perceptions of current customers, become technologically obsolete.

Discontinuous or disruptive technology presents challenges for smaller manufacturing enterprises. Enterprises founded on a specific level of technology and their entire resources consumed by exploitation or managerial efforts focused on its marketability are generally threatened with an uncertain existence. Enterprises must technologically innovate in order to compete and survive. Technology intended for a specific function in the market may be replaced with more efficient and effective technology performing the same function. Technological innovation and subsequent developments and applications in electronics, chemical processes, or medicine all represent discontinuous or disruptive technology that change how smaller manufacturing enterprises approach markets.

In some instances, smaller manufacturing enterprises are confronted with technology that is considered explosive or implosive in its behavior. Explosive technology is a radically new technology that causes conventional practices used for long time periods to be done in new ways in a very short time. Innovative and entrepreneurially driven smaller manufacturing enterprises are frequently established on concepts and approaches of explosive technology. The introduction and applications of computers represented a multidimensional revolution in many areas of human activity. Similarly, implosive technology suddenly disappears from markets and human activity. In a historical context, implosive technology may be detrimental to the health and survival of large populations. Several examples can be found in agriculture and food-processing practices where technology used was deemed unacceptable over a very short time — land cultivation, use of fertilizers, or food preservation among others.

In making decisions related to conservation, sustainability, and green strategy, managers are challenged by which level of technology to choose and how to relate it directly to green marketing strategies. Each technological level requires different management tools, approaches, and practices. The technology used to develop green marketing strategy is very much associated with the level of commitment an enterprise initially makes to green strategy.

Assessing the technological impact on current strategies and operations of smaller manufacturing enterprises is generally completed on three different levels: (1) observing how technological development will potentially impact products or services, (2) participating in innovative applications of products or services among innovators and early adopters, and (3) experimenting with technological developments in product development and letting the market decide what level of technology is acceptable at a given point in time. All assessment approaches have established methodologies in marketing research. Managers must select assessment techniques that best fit their information needs and decision-making styles.

Most smaller manufacturing enterprises handle technological challenges within their research and development activities. Given limited amounts of resources and organizational deficiencies, engineers are common proxies for research and development activities and it becomes their responsibility to monitor technological challenges. It is more likely for technological innovations to be integrated by engineers into new products or products that have the potential of being modified, to accommodate technological innovations. Due to limited financial resources, a small manufacturing enterprise will seldom adopt a new level of discontinuous or destructive technology. Either of these technology types presents an existential challenge to smaller manufacturing enterprises.

2.2.2 *Economic forces*

Economic forces introduce different challenges for smaller manufacturing enterprises. These challenges include macro-economic issues concerned with economic expansions, inflationary pressures, low unemployment, and government regulations, among others. Smaller manufacturing enterprises are vulnerable to all of them, and managers must carefully monitor these forces and understand their significance. Even the slightest changes generated by macro-economic forces may significantly alter even minor strategies. Micro-economic challenges are more related to day-to-day decisions made by managers of smaller manufacturing enterprises. They impact market behavior related to consumers, competitive issues among enterprises, allocation of resources controlled by individual enterprises, and even competitive price formations.

It is important to note that micro-economic challenges are less pressing for managers of smaller manufacturing enterprises more concerned with processes and product uniqueness or managers who attempt to promote the entire enterprise. However, managers concerned about resources and efficient and effective green marketing strategies see micro-economic challenges as relevant concerns that must be carefully evaluated and managed.

Today most managers differentiate less and less between macro- and micro-economic forces and the challenges they pose for strategic decision making. Both macro- and micro-economic forces must be carefully monitored and any relevant changes evaluated. Unfortunately, managers of smaller manufacturing enterprises tend to respond to economic forces only when necessary; this is particularly so when dealing with changes in markets and in behavior of consumers. Managers need to identify and closely monitor macro- and micro-economic developments and relate them to their marketing strategies.

2.2.3   *Social forces*

Social forces are equally important for managers of smaller manufacturing enterprises. Social forces represent a combination of ethical values leading to political climates and eventually appear as laws and regulations. Social forces guiding managers of smaller manufacturing enterprises have evolved over time and typically consist of three components — politics, ethics, and laws. Concerns over conservation, sustainability, and green strategy evolved over time. Laws and regulations are results of political and ethical interests and convictions of society.

Among smaller manufacturing enterprises, decision makers interpret social forces on two levels of managerial activities. The first is a relatively broad interpretation based on the relationships and perceptions of decision makers to society in general. How do they feel about their roles as decision makers and how do their enterprises fit into society? The second is a much more specific interpretation regarding specific implications of ethics, politics, laws, and regulations to the decision maker's proclivities? A decision maker's own perceptions, attitudes, and preferences determine the level and relevance of social forces to their entrepreneurial activities. That is how specific ethical behaviors, social norms, and laws and regulations directly impact individual enterprises.

Social forces represent the aggregate environment or social climate in which individual smaller manufacturing enterprises function as social entities. Decision makers of smaller manufacturing enterprises are guided by social forces over the short and long term and must adjust their activities to prevailing social conditions. The degree to which decision makers of smaller manufacturing enterprises subscribe to guidelines set by social forces at a given point in time varies dramatically. Decision makers differ in managerial and market behavior toward social forces and their interpretation. Decision makers may rank at different points on the ethical scale, subscribe to differing levels of political convictions, and interpret laws and regulations in the context of their own goals and objectives within the limits of laws and regulations.

Managers of smaller manufacturing enterprises make decisions consistent with prevalent social forces that directly impact their managerial abilities, guide their strategic and operational limits, and affect interactions with markets and consumers. Social forces that construct rigid strategic and operational climates for decision makers need to be constantly monitored and their importance directly related to those managerial responsibilities. The need for constant monitoring of social forces is related to contemporary issues of conservation, sustainability, and green strategy. The societal preferences for ecological issues are changing and are revealed in the ethical behavior of individuals, as part of collective social actions, and in laws and regulations that are promulgated.

Social forces are also closely connected with collective lifestyles among consumers. Societies (convene) markets, form market segments, and construct social and consumption lifestyles. Lifestyles of individual consumers differ greatly; specific patterns among consumers can be identified. These patterns of behavior directly influence markets and determine what products or services smaller manufacturing enterprise will offer.

2.2.4 *Lifestyle forces*

Lifestyles change over time and are very much subject to market fads, fashions, and trends. Fads are typically short-term phenomena that stem from groups or segments of populations that share common enthusiasm for an experience or belief. Fads at one time or another sway all population segments. Fashions are longer lasting than fads and often started by opinion leaders or innovators in population segments focusing on specific social aspects of lifestyles. Fashions are frequently identified with particular mannerisms, behaviors, or with social conformity. Fads precede fashions.

Fads and fashions shape the foundation for even longer-lasting trends. Decision makers among smaller manufacturing enterprises must be able to detect all three elements of lifestyles early and to relate their importance and significance to marketing initiatives. Fads and fashions generally serve as indicators of changing market segments. However, trends indicate changing consumer preferences and may have a direct influence on product and service offerings in the long term.

Conservation, sustainability, and even green strategy may be viewed as contemporary trends that are changing market demand for a broad variety of products and services. Each smaller manufacturing enterprise must be able to evaluate the appropriate point in time when contemporary trends will be directly relevant to their marketing strategies and when these strategies need to be converted into green marketing strategies. The issue for smaller manufacturing enterprises is when to use their monitoring and assessing of lifestyles in decision making.

Lifestyles are also influenced by actions and reactions of managers, consumers, and government regulators. Some smaller manufacturing enterprises, especially innovative high technology enterprises, compete by introducing new products or services that set fads, fashions, or trends. For example, developments in personal computer technology, application options in interconnectivity, or entertainment potentials are generally driven by managers who make decisions about what kind of technology should be introduced and how the introduction should be handled to reach the innovators and early adopters who set fads, fashions, and trends.

Consumers, on the other hand, initiate lifestyle options based on fads, fashions, and trends from the perspectives of their own preferences. Consumers decide whether a fad, fashion, or trend is appropriate to support or modify their lifestyle and to improve their level of consumption and satisfaction. Consumers can be classified based on their propensity to accept changes in their personal consumption. Propensities among consumers to accept consumption changes are closely related to how they behave in the market. Some consumers are more willing to accept changes to various degrees — innovators, early adopters, or early majority; other consumers such as late majority or laggards are less willing.

Government regulators also influence lifestyle forces. They respond to consumers and managers of smaller manufacturing enterprises and mediate positively or negatively with both. They set limits and boundaries within which both consumers and managers operate. Consumers misuse products or services in spite of managers' warnings. Managers occasionally introduce products or services that do not fully meet the needs of consumers, may harm them, or in other ways change their consumptions processes. Government regulators make the necessary adjustments between managers and consumers. In some situations, adjustments are made for the benefit of the public.

From consumer's perspectives, government regulators promulgate parameters within which consumers can safely consume products and services. Government regulators set limits and boundaries consequential to consumers' perceptions of specific products or services typically motivated by societal initiatives. Consumers may feel that a product or service is detrimental to their well-being or otherwise harms them. It is then up to managers of smaller manufacturing enterprises to respond to consumers' concerns and comply with promulgated regulations. Government regulators seldom, if ever, take the initiative to balance market relationships between managers and consumers.

Lifestyle forces are viewed as mostly devised by consumers from a marketing management perspective today. Smaller manufacturing enterprises, especially high technology enterprises under some conditions when new technology is introduced, can influence or change consumers' lifestyles. However, consumers must perceive the products and services resulting from the new technology as desirable and improving or enhancing their lifestyles in some way.

Conservation, sustainability, and green strategy are important considerations in consumers' lifestyles. Consumers are aware of them and consider them in making consumption and post-consumption decisions. Managers of smaller manufacturing enterprises must understand how consumers make these decisions. They must design and market their products and services to fit consumers' lifestyles.

2.2.5 *Integration of external forces*

The forces discussed above also have ecological dimensions. Ecology, in the form of conservation, sustainability, and green strategy, is an integral part of the environment in which smaller manufacturing enterprises function. Their decision makers must clearly understand how the factors arising from the environment in which they function impact their short- and long-term decisions. Each smaller manufacturing enterprise may comprehend the forces and incorporate them differently in their decision-making. Consequently, external forces may be perceived differently and may carry different levels of importance for each smaller manufacturing enterprise. The decision makers within each smaller manufacturing enterprise must determine the relevancy of each force to their goals and objectives.

It is important to note that interpretation of these forces differs substantially among managers with diverse backgrounds, education, and experiences such as scientists, professional managers, engineers, or financial specialists. Managers must compare their perceptions and understanding of environmental forces represented by ecological notions to those of others such as scientists and consumers. Managers of smaller manufacturing enterprises often interpret ecological forces in their relevant environment based on their own understanding of the strategic and operational goals and objectives of the enterprise. Scientific or consumer inputs into their decisions place additional burdens on managers' goals and objectives. This may require finding solutions that optimally satisfy ecological requirements in each market, but managers may not agree with the latest scientific perspectives and findings. Consumers may have higher or lower expectations of decision outcomes from managers.

Challenges confront managers of smaller manufacturing enterprises when there is agreement about ecological concerns between scientists and consumers. In these situations, additional pressure is placed on managers to comply or lose markets. Eventually, social pressures resulting from agreement between scientists and consumers may lead to laws or regulations with which managers must comply.

Managers of smaller manufacturing enterprises must keep track of rapid changes in environmental forces in expanding global markets. They must understand the environment in which they function and must be able to assess each force that directly or marginally impacts their strategic decision-making. Management of smaller manufacturing enterprises is an evolutionary process and depends on developments in the environment that an enterprise delineates as its own. Because of its specialization, know how, or its perspectives on society, environmental forces change and managers must be able to adjust to the changes. If they fail, they will not be able to function competitively.

The realization that conservation, sustainability, and green strategy, as defined by forces in the environments of smaller manufacturing enterprises, demands that managers integrate these forces into their managerial philosophies. This approach directs managers to formulate unique and competitive green marketing strategies for their products and services.

For many decision makers, among smaller manufacturing enterprises, this suggests they redefine their fundamental goals and objectives, and specify the present and future roles their products and services will assume in rapidly changing global markets must be a part of their new managerial philosophy. For some managers, this necessity encourages them to formulate new goals and objectives that include public's notion of green strategy.

Each smaller manufacturing enterprise must formulate a methodology which will enable the enterprise to gather the necessary information needed to make proprietary strategic decisions in the context of an ecological framework — specifically green marketing strategies. In other words, societal and consumers' concerns with conservation, sustainability, and green strategy must be clearly understood by managers of smaller manufacturing enterprises and must be related to their own green marketing strategies.

2.3   Commitment to Green Strategy

Consumers globally are very much aware of the need for conservation and sustainability. In consumers' opinions, conservation and sustainability must naturally lead to green strategy. Some consumers are adjusting their consumption habits and lifestyles to consume more green products and use more green services. These adjustments result in subtle lifestyle changes that may not be detected by managers of less dynamic, smaller manufacturing enterprises. It is apparent on the global level that consumers drive ecological concerns and influence market conditions for green products and services. These developments challenge managers of smaller manufacturing enterprises to formulate green marketing strategies and introduce green products and services.

Managers of smaller manufacturing enterprises must decide how committed they are to green strategy. They must decide how this broad societal notion of green strategy translates into proprietary green marketing strategies. Each smaller manufacturing enterprise interprets green strategy differently and formulates its green marketing strategies accordingly. These inevitable decisions are made because consumers' concerns about conservation, sustainability, and green strategy as social trends are growing.

The commitment to green marketing strategies is complex and resource intensive for most decision makers of smaller manufacturing enterprises. The commitment to is the result of understanding of how external forces shape various aspects of marketing initiatives. This understanding is vital and determines the intensity of the commitment to green strategy and eventual formulation of an enterprise's own green marketing strategies.

The commitment to green strategy represents the evolution of the internal strategic philosophy for each smaller manufacturing enterprise. The new internal strategic philosophy impacts how an enterprise approaches markets and how it communicates with its customers and the public. Green-marketing strategies must carry a message, sent through a comprehensive communication channel that clearly states the degree to which an enterprise is committed to not only green strategy, but also green marketing strategies in total.

Commitments to green marketing strategies indicate more direct and articulate communication processes between smaller manufacturing enterprises and the public. Managers must send clear and concise messages stating what they want to communicate and provide justification. The public is obligated to articulate their inquiries, criticisms, or concerns without prejudice. Given the diversity of public interest groups and their socio-political orientations, articulating their intentions may not be always possible.

It is increasingly important to realize that the public eventually judges how committed an enterprise is to green strategy as embedded in ecological notions of society. Managers of smaller manufacturing enterprises must decide how committed they are to green strategy. For some managers, this is a strategic decision because the level of commitment will have a direct influence on implementation of green marketing strategies and future marketing activities. Regardless of how strong the commitment is, it must be communicated to the public through overt marketing initiatives.

The commitment to green strategy is the driving force for managers of smaller manufacturing enterprises. They must understand the external forces that shape their green marketing strategies. They must formulate their missions and be able to communicate them to consumers and the public. Managers of smaller manufacturing enterprises must also examine their resources and decide how strong their commitment to green strategy can be.

If smaller manufacturing enterprises commit to ecological trends shaping consumer markets, their commitment to green strategy will impact their financial, human, and physical resources. In order to include green dimensions, managers may have to consider creatively financing their marketing activities, train or hire specialist with green skills, and insure their physical resources such as manufacturing lines and distribution systems are consistent with green marketing activities. This may be an expensive and time-consuming process for some smaller manufacturing enterprises.

2.4   Resources

Resource availability determines the level of commitment to green strategy among smaller manufacturing enterprises. Each enterprise has a different mix of resources and ability to generate resources. Enterprises can generate resources internally through its marketing activities by being profitable and externally by presenting a favorable image to society. Some enterprises maintain adequate financial assets, while others have technologically sophisticated staff or maintain physical resources that enable them to produce or deliver a variety of products or services. The level of commitment to green strategy may be based on one or all three resources that make up a resource base.

If a smaller manufacturing enterprise lacks the necessary resources to commit to green strategy, it is possible to source resources externally. An enterprise may source for necessary capital to commit to green strategy because green strategy is considered a favorable global socio-economic trend and investors are willing to invest in it. Managers and specialist skilled in green issues can be employed or otherwise engaged for complex green challenges. Industrial parks around the world offer green facilities to manufacture green products or offer green services.

Each smaller manufacturing enterprise needs to determine which resource is most important to the level of commitment the enterprise is willing to make. Many managers suggest that making a commitment to green strategy is costly and requires major expenditures and that smaller enterprises generally do not have sufficient internal capital to make the commitment. Smaller enterprises that have unique technological or innovative approaches to green strategy are successful in sourcing the necessary capital from outside. The availability of other resources not only depends on availability of financial resources but also on managerial abilities and innovativeness. If managers of an enterprise want to commit to green strategy and have a compelling reason, they will find ways through cooperation with other enterprises to fulfill their commitment.

2.4.1 *Financial*

Managers of smaller manufacturing enterprise consider financial resources as a combination of current assets, cash reserves, ability to raise capital, and ability to borrow. Each component represents a different level of perceived risk and strategic impact for an enterprise. Current assets are considered reserves, and turn into an available financial resource only if decision makers consider them to be at a low risk level. Cash reserves are considered as temporary and typically not used for major new marketing initiatives.

For some smaller manufacturing enterprises, a commitment to green strategy is a form of diversification and the enterprise that has sufficient available capital or can raise it from outside sources. The ability to raise capital from outside sources requires documentation supported by an innovative approach to justify diversification such as a commitment to green strategy. An enterprise may borrow the amount needed depending on the level of commitment to green strategy and the time period associated with the breakeven point when the results of the commitment to green strategy will offset the expenditure. These are managerial decisions that need to be made in the context of the marketing activities necessary to enter the market place.

2.4.2 *Human*

The level of commitment to green strategy by smaller manufacturing enterprises generally depends on availability of managerial and functional interest or expertise associated with green marketing issues. Thus, managers decide if there is sufficient internal interest or expertise in green issues, and if the enterprise is capable of formulating successful green strategies. More dynamic enterprises tend to judge the level of their commitment to green strategy in terms of what additional human resources are necessary to formulate innovative green strategies.

Managers of smaller manufacturing enterprises view human resources as representing five basic areas: marketing management, financial management, engineering, research and development capacity, and scientific and technical capabilities. Depending on the size of an enterprise, the number of individuals with various degrees of expertise in any one or several of these areas may vary. For example, the manager of a small enterprise specializing in fabrication of production equipment may have an engineering background or an advanced academic degree in management specializing in research and development.

A larger multidepartment manufacturing enterprise marketing several lines of consumer products, based on advanced chemical processes, may have a staff of chemists conducting research and developing new products. It may also have an engineering department specializing in installing and maintaining chemistry-related production lines and may also operate a scientific research laboratory conducting pure and applied research. These functions, including marketing and financial management, must be staffed with suitable and experienced personnel.

If a smaller manufacturing enterprise commits to green strategy, existing staff may have to be trained in the process of how green strategy in its broad interpretation is transformed into successful green marketing strategies. If an enterprise does not have the necessary personnel to implement green marketing strategies, it needs to hire them, or in some extreme case, outsource them. In today's technologically diverse world specializations such as pure or applied research in any scientific discipline can be contracted to a laboratory. Product research, modification, or redesign can all be contracted out. Smaller manufacturing enterprises with limited human resources have flexibility in obtaining the necessary activities from outside.

Smaller manufacturing enterprises may be able to cooperate with an institution of higher learning on formulation of green marketing strategies and varied aspects of product or service development. Small business development centers administered by university faculties work closely with smaller manufacturing enterprises and encourage university faculty to assist in development of optimal green marketing strategies consistent with the managerial philosophy of an enterprise.

2.4.3 *Physical*

Commitment to green strategy is dependent on the availability of physical resources. It is difficult for smaller manufacturing enterprises to implement green strategy if they do not have the necessary facilities and equipment to manufacture green products or deliver green services. Consistent with the many options available today, managers of such enterprises may choose to invest in physical resources or outsource them. The ability to successfully manage physical resources and use them in formulating green marketing strategies depends on a manager's ability and skills. It is more likely that physical resources in larger enterprises will be managed internally and will be outsourced only in special instances. Smaller manufacturing enterprises often cluster their physical resources.

From marketing and financial management perspectives, physical resources include several distinct categories. Each category includes capabilities and functions closely aligned with how products are developed, manufactured, and marketed and the availability of physical facilities such as production lines, warehouses, and transportation to move products as they are produced, stored, and eventually delivered to consumers.

Smaller manufacturing enterprises must be able to develop, test, and distribute products and services. The facilities used for such tasks range from small engineering laboratories and design centers to fully staffed product development departments with the equipment necessary to develop and test safe products or services. Temporary storage and longer-term warehousing facilities are also needed. Facilities may be located as needed depending on space availability, financial resources, and other circumstances. Some enterprises prefer to locate these facilities away from their manufacturing and service facilities or management centers in order to maintain creativity and originality.

Most smaller manufacturing enterprises manufacture their own products and deliver services; consequently, manufacturing and service facilities are typically also the centers of all managerial and marketing operations. Manufacturing and service facilities represent the entire scope of operations necessary to manufacture and move a product to the market or provide complete services. Most enterprises generally operate their manufacturing and service facilities to capacity. If additional capacity is needed, expansion of existing facilities may be problematic because of either a lack of financial resources or availability of location. When major new marketing initiatives are planned, an enterprise will often expand its manufacturing and service facilities elsewhere. New manufacturing facilities may be needed to assure conditions consistent with green marketing strategies if the commitment of an enterprise to green marketing is strong.

Expansion of manufacturing and service facilities is relatively complex and driven by market and growth expectations. Responding to market expansions or otherwise motivated growth of an enterprise means a major reorientation that must be financially justified. Expansions of manufacturing and service facilities may be influenced by local economic and political decisions. When smaller manufacturing enterprises plan an expansion, local municipalities may offer incentives, subsidies, or even long-term leases just to keep such enterprises. A municipality or other entity may offer complete new facilities in expectation of job creation, increased tax revenue, or local development.

Smaller manufacturing enterprises maintain after-sales and technical support facilities. Such facilities may take several forms to maintain relationships between consumers and markets. After-sales service typically deals with marketing issues necessary to maintain high satisfaction among consumers such as merchandise return or replacement services. Technical support facilities perform repairs, adjustments, or other services connected with mechanical or technical issues. Some enterprises manage both facilities on location, while others use separate locations. Both after-sales service and technical support services must expand as product or service sales increase along with manufacturing output.

Logistical and distribution facilities are also major concerns for smaller manufacturing enterprises. These include storage, warehousing, and transportation facilities. Temporary storage such as manufactured inventory facilities are generally located adjacent to manufacturing; warehousing facilities may be located elsewhere or contracted out as are transportation needs. For some enterprises, logistical and distribution facilities represent both investment and expenses depending on how an enterprise decides to manage the logistical and distribution requirements for its products and support its services.

Small manufacturing enterprises are challenged by the concerns over post-consumption issues to develop facilities for used products and recycling. Accepting products for refurbishing and recycling forces enterprises to establish additional facilities. According to consumers and the public interest in green strategy issues, enterprises must take responsibility for products and services from their inception to the end of its psychological, social, and economic life. This new outlook on consumption is motivating enterprises to build new facilities and offer new services closely connected with their green products and services.

Smaller manufacturing enterprises find this development challenging and seek new approaches as part of their solutions to these challenges. Some enterprises have developed separate facilities, while others tend to contract out for post-consumption facilities. Although post-consumption and recycling facilities will assume a greater role in the entire marketing process in the future, enterprises still view these facilities as unnecessary and frequently rely on secondary markets to satisfy consumers' demand for these services. Less proactive enterprises with a low commitment to green strategy tend to perceive post-consumption and recycling facilities as a financial burden and are not interested in making investments in post-consumption and recycling facilities.

2.4.4 *Resource availability*

Managers of smaller manufacturing enterprises must consider their resource base as part of the decision to commit to green strategy. Each enterprise manages a different resource base and values it differently. Managers of smaller manufacturing enterprises expect that accepting green strategy as a major force in society and committing to it will require additional resources. The resource base for most enterprises will change. Some enterprises will need additional financial resources while other enterprises will have to learn how to become green and may have to hire specialists to fulfill their commitment to green strategy. The question of physical resources can be solved in most cases. The main issue is how drastically will the resource base change?

Resource availability among smaller manufacturing enterprises is a managerial dilemma. Many smaller manufacturing enterprises limit their marketing capabilities to a few products or services. Every time an enterprise adds a new product or offers a new service it considers that a major expansion in its marketing activities and a drain on resources. Introducing green products or services drains resources. Managers must develop accurate tools and techniques to understand how green products or services will drain resources and how the depleted resources will be replaced.

2.5 Mission Statement

When the managers of a smaller manufacturing enterprise reach a level of commitment to green marketing strategy, its mission must be defined or redefined, whatever the case may be. A clearly articulated mission statement represents a path of historical evolution, current market orientation, and future strategic direction. A mission summarizes the evolutionary path of an enterprise and anticipates its future strategic aim. It defines continuity, direction, and managerial responsibilities of an enterprise in case of existential difficulties or discontinuities due to unexpected succession concerns or market failures.

A mission statement consists of three fundamental parts on which smaller manufacturing enterprises are founded: core competencies in the form of managerial skills and expectations; focus on consumers and markets; and ability to innovate and grow and, for some, to survive in the future. The three fundamental parts of a mission statement can be somewhat abstract and ambiguous for managers of some of the smaller manufacturing enterprises. Such enterprises may have been founded on a simple one-product idea and, during their growth, they focused on product modifications and improvements without any significant market connotation. A green dimension to a product or service may merely require adding a new ingredient or changing the manufacturing process. The basic mission of an enterprise may not change if its commitment to green strategy requires only minor changes in a product or service or how it is manufactured. For a high-technology enterprise, integrating a green strategy may represent another level of technology which may require a major move along its technology curve. This is a primary reason why all three elements of a mission statement must be examined individually but considered as a total.

2.5.1   *Core competencies*

Core competencies are determined and set by the original founders of smaller manufacturing enterprises based on their vision transformed into managerial, marketing, and technological knowledge. If an enterprise changes its core competencies or modifies them for a rational reason such as including a green focus in its mission, it will change or modify its core competencies. This is a major task and may require approvals and consensus among top management. If core competencies are altered, targeted consumers, market segments, and markets may shift.

Consumers interested in green issues will have slightly different interests than the original consumers serviced by an enterprise. Market segments may have to be redefined to include a green emphasis which also suggests that the overall market for green products and services must be redefined. Consequently, an enterprise must be able to innovate with emphasis on green products and services. In some instances, a new focus on innovative activities frequently changes the overall market direction, for example, from low-technology to high-technology applications. For some smaller manufacturing enterprises, this change in innovative activities may require not only a change in its technological sophistication, but also place a greater burden on new product and service development.

An enterprise mission statement provides a framework for its core managerial and technical skills, knowledge, and abilities. Every smaller manufacturing enterprise is made up of managers, technicians, and other specialists with different abilities and expectations. This combination of managers, technical, and other specialists combined with distinct sets of financial and physical resources makes up core competencies. Core competencies are frequently perceived as the founding principles of an enterprise and provide the fundamental component of a mission statement.

In technologically evolving and highly competitive markets, core competencies improve over time to reflect external environmental conditions and growing market sophistication. A mission statement must have the flexibility to anticipate developments leading to evolutionary expansion of core competencies. An enterprise founded on manual technology intended for custom fabrication of products or equipment may, because of managerial leadership and foresight, evolve into a supplier of automation technology for large manufacturers.

Some smaller manufacturing enterprises suggest that core competencies do not change over time, are reflected in the managerial style of the enterprise, and the internal culture or mentoring abilities of top management pass on core values. The alternate position suggests that core values evolve as an enterprise learns from the environment around it. Consumers may ask for technologically new products or technological improvements to existing products. Suppliers may offer components, parts, or accessories representing technological improvements. Other external stakeholders may try to influence managers of external developments important to their products or services. The core values of an enterprise may change as new knowledge is acquired.

Core competencies may change as new managers and functional specialists are hired due to the evolution of knowledge, education, and scientific advancements. Advances in managerial skills and techniques have contributed to major knowledge improvements among managers of smaller manufacturing enterprises. Technical knowledge among scientists and engineers in charge of new product or service development has grown considerably and has had a direct impact on the marketing abilities of enterprises.

2.5.2   *Consumers and markets*

A modified focus on consumers, market segments, and markets because of a new green commitment also has great implications for a mission statement. Consumers may be fragmented into many groups because of their preferences. Consumer groups that prefer green products and services may require different levels of marketing activities and expect a different array of marketing support services. For example, adding a green component to a product may require additional support during the purchase and consumption of a product. Consumers may ask for direct support for disposal of a product at the end its useful life. A comprehensive mission statement must address such fundamentally new consumer preferences. Markets also change and must be redefined when consumer preferences change.

A clearly defined focus on consumers, market segments, and markets is another component of a mission statement typical of smaller manufacturing enterprises and is closely aligned with core competencies. Identifying potential consumers, segmenting markets, and defining primary markets consistent with the core competencies of an enterprise are major tasks. The abilities of enterprise managers to define and select products and services depends on how well they understand their core competencies and how skilled they are in channeling them into profitable markets.

Market profitability largely depends on how attractive the products and services developed and marketed based on core competencies of an enterprise are to consumers. For smaller manufacturing enterprises, a mission statement specifies relationships and stabilities between markets and core competencies. For many low-technology, smaller manufacturing enterprises, market definition results from managers' strategic efforts to apply the knowledge and abilities of an enterprise to interpret core competencies and present them as products and services.

Consumers look for products and services that satisfy their consumption processes and support their lifestyles. They form market segments and drive demand for specific products and services. Their combined demand for similar products or services with distinct consumption characteristics forms markets. Consumers initiate demand for products and services that they understand and know how to consume. They respond to product and service offerings that are often functions of collective social actions, such as current fashions, even though they may not fully understand their functional or technological complexity.

The relationship between core competencies and markets present a complex dilemma for high-technology, smaller manufacturing enterprises that introduce revolutionary technology that has the potential to disturb existing markets. There might be numerous applications for their unique new technology based on their core competencies. Managers face a quandary as to which version of the technology should be introduced and how to define the market for it. Different applications may represent different markets. It is up to the managers to evaluate the risk factors related to consumers' acceptance of each application.

2.5.3   *Ability to innovate*

The ability to innovate is another component of a mission statement. The ability to innovate is a complex issue for many smaller manufacturing enterprises with financial, managerial, and technological challenges. Some enterprises can modify a product or service, but lack the ability to develop a new product or service because product or service development requires investment or skilled personnel and they lack one or both. A complete understanding of consumers' needs related to market dynamics is also required. Smaller, single product, or service-oriented manufacturing enterprises generally lack these essential requirements. Larger enterprises have the necessary resources for innovative activities even though some green initiatives may completely change their original mission. In some instances, especially among high technology enterprises, managers may obtain the necessary resources from outside sources. Lack of innovative abilities or changes in current innovative activities may have a major impact on commitment to green strategy.

A mission statement for smaller manufacturing enterprises must also address how and when to invest in innovative activities generally defined as creative innovation. Enterprises may choose to innovate over time by continually improving products or services, offering the latest prevailing technology, and addressing the benefits of improved products. Other enterprises may choose to invest in innovation on a project basis. There is a compelling need to innovate whenever products or services are no longer in demand, competitive pressures intensify, or market conditions change dramatically.

Sources of innovation among smaller manufacturing enterprises may be internal or external. Some enterprises have the necessary human, financial, and physical resources to innovate internally, while others are forced to outsource innovation. In most cases, smaller manufacturing enterprises do not maintain separate research and development functions dedicated to innovative activities. Most enterprises maintain technical functions such as engineering or manufacturing support. Some owner managers, especially in startup enterprises, may have sufficient scientific or engineering expertise to introduce innovative activities leading to major product or service improvements.

Externally sourced innovation may lead to marketing and competitive conflicts. The supplier may not fully understand the mission of the enterprise or marketing specialists are not able to communicate the key element of the intended innovation. Such conflicts may result in products or services that are not fully consistent with their markets, thereby reducing competitive advantage and profitability.

The ability to innovate requires a combination of financial, human, and physical resources for smaller manufacturing enterprises that must be optimally balanced. It requires clear direction — a mandate from top management that must specify the parameters for any innovation. Top decision makers must set the limits of how much and what kind of innovation is necessary to meet the demands of their consumers.

2.5.4 *The need to formulate a mission statement*

Substantial changes in any of the three fundamental constructs of a mission statement require redefinition of a mission statement. A commitment to green strategy and subsequent implementation of green marketing strategies represent substantial changes for smaller manufacturing enterprises in managerial philosophy, organizational structure, and future marketing initiatives. Furthermore, a commitment to green marketing strategies changes not only an enterprise's mission but also impacts its consumers, market segments, and markets.

Some managers suggest that mission statements among smaller manufacturing enterprises are formulated by top decision makers based on multidisciplinary consensus. Depending on the size of an enterprise, there is little capacity for consensus, especially if an enterprise is managed by a key decision maker or an owner–manager. In such situations, the owner–manager is responsible for formulating a mission statement frequently with internal and sometimes external assistance from management advisers or consultants. Most smaller manufacturing enterprises committed to green marketing strategies often need knowledgeable functional managers able to assist them with mission statement formulation.

In today's competitive global markets, it is essential that every enterprise, regardless of its size and who manages it, must have a clear understanding of what its mission is and how to guide its market presence. Managers and personnel need to know what their enterprise represents and the core values driving its market presence. Consumers want to know more about the enterprises whose products or services they consume in current and transparent Internet-based global markets. Consumers want transparency especially from enterprises that promote green products or services.

2.6   Closing Comments

Commitments by smaller manufacturing enterprises to green marketing strategies are major events and differ significantly in their intensity. Some enterprises are relatively passive in their commitment, while others are proactive and completely change their market focus. Contemporary global market trends clearly indicate that concerns over conservation, sustainability, and green strategy are driven by social perspectives that eventually change markets for consumer products and services.

Decision makers of smaller manufacturing enterprises must respond to challenges that originate from social or market changes. They are responsible for setting the intensity of their commitment to green issues in society and their markets. Their commitment is based on understanding the external forces affecting their enterprise and how these forces challenge their marketing initiatives. They must understand how available resources can be restructured or expanded for reaching their green marketing strategies. Finally, they must redefine or formulate a mission statement that corresponds to their intensity of commitment to green marketing strategies.

In today's global markets and with the strong Internet influence on consumers, managers of smaller manufacturing enterprises must be able to develop green products and services with strong consumers' inputs. They must develop green marketing strategies that not only deliver green products and services to consumers, but which also effectively communicate what their products or service represent in green markets and the environments that shape these markets. And finally, managers must communicate with their customers and the public concerned with green issues.

Recommended Readings

1. Cramer, A. and Karabell, Z. (2010). *Sustainable Excellence: The Future in a Fast-Changing World* (© by authors, distributed by Macmillan, New York, NY).
2. Kotler, P. and Armstrong, G. (2016). *Principles of Marketing*, Global Edition (Pearson Education Limited, Essex, UK).
3. Schuacher, E. F. (1973). *Small is Beautiful: Economics as if People Mattered* (Perennial Library, Harper & Row, Publishers, New York, NY).

Chapter 3

Enterprise Action, Marketing Management, and Green Marketing Strategies

Managers of smaller manufacturing enterprises face demand for green products and services from a variety of public sources, but mainly from consumers. Demand for green products and services is typically expressed in the broad context of green strategy. Green strategy as perceived by the public is not clearly defined and is a major challenge for managers of many smaller manufacturing enterprises. Consumers have clear perceptions and definitions of what a green strategy ought to be — a rational utilization of societal and enterprise resources, particularly energy. Consumers expect managers of smaller manufacturing enterprises to respond to their challenges, which in practice mean redefinition and modification of marketing initiatives. Managers must develop an understanding of what green strategy represents for their marketing initiatives. A commitment to green strategy for smaller manufacturing enterprises, as defined by the public and consumers, requires major changes often leading to reexamination of objectives and goals and, more specifically, marketing strategies.

Developing green marketing strategies is not a simple task. Depending on the makeup of enterprise's products and services, green marketing strategies may impact the entire structure, its managerial philosophy, and most of all, its marketing orientation. Managers need to develop new outlooks on green marketing strategies and their consequences as smaller manufacturing enterprises begin to change.

Managers typically look for new opportunities, develop products or services, and market them; they search for more systematic ways to manage and formulate marketing strategies. Managers must clearly understand the opportunities and challenges of green strategy.

Adoption of marketing management as a managerial philosophy becomes a necessity as smaller manufacturing enterprises grow. Marketing management is a systematic approach to how marketing managers identify, evaluate, and implement marketing opportunities. It provides a framework for marketing action and gives managers a more structured approach for developing green products and services including an objective way of formulating green marketing strategies.

3.1   Enterprise Action

Commitment to green marketing strategies by managers of smaller manufacturing enterprises is a major event that dramatically changes market focus. The decision to commit to green marketing initiatives is preceded by strategic considerations ranging from questions of how such a commitment will impact future actions of the entire enterprise, but more specifically how the commitment will change the mission, management style, organizational structure, and, most of all, key markets and consumers. Answers to these questions depend on the size of an enterprise, how it is managed, and its willingness to become green.

Even when an enterprise commits to green marketing initiates and develops green marketing strategies for its product or services, its success of becoming green depends on its resources and managerial skills. Some smaller manufacturing enterprises do not have the necessary resources to sustain their commitment to green marketing initiatives. Their financial resources, or the ability to obtain them, may not be sufficient for the necessary investment. Managerial skills and propensity to face change may be sufficient or even substantial. Other smaller manufacturing enterprises may have the necessary prerequisites to become green but lack determination.

Decision makers among smaller manufacturing enterprises may perceive changes related to green marketing strategies as major challenges and are not willing to confront them. They may choose to be relatively passive in internalizing green issues. From the perspective of marketing management, such enterprises perform minimum marketing activities, and most likely offer a limited number of products or services. The focus is generally on fabrication of customized products or services based on specialized skills that are managed by product or service specialists, ranging from skilled craftsmen to scientists, who offer to deliver unique products or services based on innovative technology. Such individuals with strong entrepreneurial tendencies, driven by scientific knowledge and intuitive marketing abilities, become aware of green issues though their customers, clients, or consumers and only modify their products or services when required to meet green expectations.

Even marginally committed smaller manufacturing enterprises consider options and decide how extensively they want to commit resources and managerial talents to green issues. If they commit resources, they then decide how to supplement marketing activities with green initiatives. For example, managers of smaller manufacturing enterprises decide how much to invest and what specialists, if any, must be assigned or hired to assist with green issues. Marginally committed smaller manufacturing enterprises tend to systematically adjust as needed to consumers' preferences and changing market demand to optimize market positions. Over time and only as necessary, they acquire the essential resources needed to reach the level of commitment consistent with green consumer demand.

When decision makers of smaller manufacturing enterprises consider green options and adjust marketing activities to correspond to the green demands of customers, they first modify existing marketing strategies to meet consumer demands. The modifications may range from product adjustments to meet green consumers' expectations to major restructuring or revamping of manufacturing processes. Among smaller manufacturing enterprises, these developments are preceded by adjustments in attitudes toward green challenges among decision makers and managers.

The managerial changes that follow lead to adjustments in managerial philosophy, resource allocation, and marketing strategy.

Managers gradually seek marketing opportunities and develop approaches consistent with the green standards around them. The green standards around them are predictably initiated by consumers and reflected in market demand; these green standards are often impelled by competitors and occasionally legislatively mandated depending on the strength and relevancy of outside forces.

A smaller manufacturing enterprise's commitment to green marketing strategies impacts external as well as internal marketing strategies and operations. External marketing activities are modified around perceptions of consumers, competitors, and even regulators. The objective is to be perceived more favorably publicly. Internally, marketing goals and objectives also change; managers and even employees become advocates for green products and services and articulate uniform commitment to green issues.

The entire enterprise needs to accept the new green commitment. It is necessary for managers and employees to articulate the commitment to green issues made by decision makers, and management and employees must understand the commitment equally. The enterprise changes its overall managerial mode once the new commitment is accepted and begins to perceive consumers as the center of marketing initiatives. The new mode of marketing initiatives is reflected in managerial approaches and practices resulting in strategic marketing management.

3.2 Marketing Management

The practice of marketing management among smaller manufacturing enterprises represents a relatively new approach to managerial decision-making. It is a form of managerial philosophy that changes the overall marketing focus from an emphasis on production, sales, or distribution to an emphasis on consumers and users. Marketing management is considered a strategic tool by more-advanced smaller manufacturing enterprises whose leadership recognizes consumers and users as the ultimate focal points for marketing initiatives. From a managerial perspective, marketing management provides a systematic approach to identification and selection of opportunities in the market place and offers qualitative and quantitative approaches to evaluating and selecting optimal marketing opportunities. Marketing management also provides a framework for entrepreneurial approaches to implementing optimal marketing opportunities, building an organizational structure for optimal marketing opportunities, and implementing and eventually controlling them.

Marketing management provides analytical tools for identifying and selecting marketing initiatives that foster exchanges, relationships, and networks with consumers, users, and markets. The concepts, approaches, and even theories formulated by marketing management also provide planning options for implementing product or service exchanges, customer or user relationships, and participating in marketing networks. Finally, marketing management provides the mechanisms for control of marketing approaches ranging from quality control from conception to after consumption practices of products and services.

Marketing management offers innovative and growing smaller manufacturing enterprises a new managerial philosophy and a framework within which smaller manufacturing enterprises can make their decisions and the decision makers and marketing managers can better realize marketing opportunities. Commitment to green marketing initiatives represents challenges that can be resolved within a marketing management framework. The most important aspect of marketing management is the realization that consumers are the focal points of green marketing initiatives; this realization provides smaller manufacturing enterprises with initiatives for formulating green marketing strategies.

Many creative managerial approaches to green marketing strategies are entrenched in marketing management. Within the framework of marketing management, managers help implement the commitment to green products and services and move marketing initiatives and actions to a new level. These changes are particularly important for smaller and less dynamic manufacturing enterprises that are unaware of marketing management as a managerial philosophy or are reluctant to adopt it because of the background of top decision makers. A major event such as a commitment to green issues presents an opportunity for an enterprise to introduce marketing management along with new levels of consumer orientation.

3.3   Green Marketing Strategies

Green marketing strategies can be implemented by smaller manufacturing enterprises on different levels depending on the market behavior of its products or services, competitive pressures in the market, and environmental conditions combined with managerial characteristics of the enterprise. Green strategies as perceived by the public can be interpreted differently by individual smaller manufacturing enterprises and may produce a variety of responses on the distinct levels of an enterprise. This may be the case when green marketing strategies are interpreted in a broad context of the market, competition, and environment that present different options and interpretation.

For some smaller manufacturing enterprises, green marketing strategies may imply changing the entire organizational and strategic structure of an enterprise after systematic reexamination of current operations. An enterprise may completely reposition itself from a traditional production, sales, distribution, or marketing orientation to a new green enterprise. From this point on, the enterprise functions with a total focus on green initiatives, green marketing strategies, and green products and services. All resources lead to development and marketing of green products and services. In some instances, this approach calls for a fundamental change in the mission of the enterprise.

Some smaller manufacturing enterprises do not have the resources and managerial abilities to commit to the broadest interpretation of green strategies as defined by the public. Instead, they attempt to become green by focusing on marketing activities. Such enterprises deploy green marketing strategies within the framework of marketing management. Their green orientation begins with identifying and assessing green marketing opportunities. Optimal green marketing opportunities are ranked on factors such as potential consumer demand, rate of market penetration, potential market demand, expected life of a product or service, and most important, long-term profitability. If the decision to exploit optimal opportunities is made, skilled specialists and managers are appointed, and an organizational structure is finalized, then green products or services are developed and introduced to the market, appropriate controls instituted, and market performance of green products or services is measured periodically.

The marketing management approach to developing green marketing strategies does not imply that a smaller manufacturing enterprise will focus only on green products or services. It is very likely that an enterprise will market several lines of products or services and green products or services will supplement them. If the new green line is profitable and strategically beneficial, some smaller manufacturing enterprises may transition from the traditional products or services to the more profitable green lines. A few smaller manufacturing enterprises eventually decide to separate green lines from traditional lines and start a new venture dedicated only to green products or services.

Another approach utilized by smaller manufacturing enterprises concerns only individual products or services. In response to demands from consumers or markets, occasionally because of competition, managers will evaluate converting or modifying a product or service to be positioned in the market as green. Such conversions or modifications in the context of public interpretation of green strategy only appear to be a temporary measure. Product or service conversions or modifications can be completed on several levels. A product or service can be redesigned to include new green components, it may be modified to perform a green task, or instructions may be rewritten indicating how it can be used safely in a green environment.

Formulation of green marketing strategies and relating them to the broad social perception of green strategy is a complex process and depends on the willingness and commitment of smaller manufacturing enterprises' marketing managers. Each enterprise is responsible for its own decision to become green. However, the decision to become green is dependent not only on the commitment to become green, but also on the availability of resources within and outside the enterprise. To a degree, this is also a function of the managerial philosophy and abilities of top managers managing smaller manufacturing enterprises. Top decision makers with craftsman-like tendencies, if they are willing to commit to green initiatives, will most likely modify a product or service to achieve the effect expected by clients. Those interested in promoting an enterprise along with products and services will likely redesign products and services including manufacturing processes to be green, and occasionally supplement green initiatives to existing activities. This is because top decision makers with entrepreneurial tendencies and strong interest in promoting their enterprises need to demonstrate that their enterprises operate at the forefront of socially significant forces. However, top decision makers who rationally allocate their resources and optimize their market positions are more likely to develop new green products or services and manufacture them on modern green equipment consistent with their commitment level to green marketing strategies and subject to their interpretation of green strategy as defined by the public.

Introduction of green products and services by smaller manufacturing enterprises consistent with a broad public definition of green strategy is a difficult managerial balancing act. Marketing managers must balance green consumers' perceptions of green products and services, often filtered through a broad public definition of green strategy, with consumer satisfaction. If consumers are not satisfied with the green products or services offered to them, they will not purchase them. Thus, the broad societal perceptions and interpretations of green strategy provide a framework for managers of smaller manufacturing enterprises and each top decision maker must define what it means for their own marketing initiatives. The marketing management approach provides the most acceptable approach to dealing with these challenges.

3.4 Domestic and International Green Initiatives

Green consumer markets are not confined to one region of the world, but are all over the world. The global character of green markets presents challenges for smaller manufacturing enterprises involved in international marketing activities. Many of these challenges depend on how their domestic markets relate to the markets around them. The connections between domestic and foreign markets among smaller manufacturing enterprises ranges from exporting initiatives to complex direct investments in foreign markets with several contractual arrangements in between.

Depending on the commitment to green activities that top decision makers of smaller manufacturing enterprises make, they may manage different levels of green commitment in each market. Some marketing managers suggest that approaches to green initiatives in various markets depend on the green consumer demand in each market. For some smaller manufacturing enterprises, the commitment to green initiatives is important in the home market but not in markets abroad. Domestic consumer demand requires a supply of green products and services but foreign consumers may not. The dilemma for marketing managers is whether it is profitable and socially responsible not to offer for green products or services in their foreign markets if the demand for them does not exist in those markets.

Marketing managers of smaller manufacturing enterprises who manage with opportunistic expectations often manage a portfolio of markets with different levels of green demand and commitments. They may not differentiate between domestic and foreign markets. The portfolio of green markets may be arranged on potential and existing green market demand and long-term profitability. Long-term profitability is subject to the managers' assessments. In these situations, top decision makers provide performance guidelines and offer green products and services accordingly. A number of managers among smaller manufacturing enterprises point out that for some global markets the difference between green products or services and conventional ones is minimal, others suggest that green products of services need to match consumers' needs in each market.

The portfolio approach to marketing green products and services in global markets is overwhelming for many smaller manufacturing enterprises and suited more for enterprises with diverse marketing strategies — strategies designed for specific markets. However, a significant number of smaller manufacturing enterprises operate in global markets using different modes of market entry and ownership styles. Marketing managers in these situations have more flexibility to develop or modify and otherwise allocate green products and services among markets.

Smaller manufacturing enterprises fully committed to broad societal interpretation of green strategy do not necessarily differentiate between domestic and foreign markets or among international markets. They fully commit to their own unique definition of green marketing strategy and they do not differentiate marketing activities from market to market, although demand for green products or services may fluctuate among the markets. Sometimes, such smaller manufacturing enterprises are criticized by local green activists that they overemphasize green products and services in some markets and underemphasize them in others. Only a few smaller manufacturing enterprises gauge green products and services exactly to the green needs of consumers in specific markets.

There appears to be a distinct need for commitments to broad green strategy to differ between domestic and international markets for some smaller manufacturing enterprises. If differences between markets exist, it is likely because of technological attributes of products and services. Internationally, product attributes — functional, physical, or psychological — are subject to regulations, certification, or other administrative controls. Products and services for some international markets may need to be designed exclusively, while they can be modified for other markets. In the early stages of exporting from one country to another, products may not be modified except for obvious technical or cultural differences, such as energy inputs or color preferences. This is particularly apparent in export operations between technologically advanced markets and technologically challenged markets.

3.4.1 *Green commitments to domestic markets*

Managers of smaller manufacturing enterprises make commitments to green issues because of internal or external challenges and administrative directives. Enterprises may be challenged externally by changing market condition, competitors, or environmental conditions. They may be challenged internally by lower sales revenue, lack of green products or services, or lack of managerial interest by top decision makers. Occasionally, a change in top management or adding a functional specialist such as a green-oriented marketing specialist may bring about commitment to green issues. It is difficult to identify specific sources or motivations in responses to green challenges because they differ from one enterprise to another.

In order to compete in markets that emphasize green issues, smaller manufacturing enterprises must meet green challenges that are integral to their missions and represent core competitive advantages. Managerial philosophies must be consistent with individual missions, highlighting their technological and marketing competitive advantages. Green market performance must signal a core competitive advantage reinforced by technological and marketing knowledge.

From a managerial perspective, addressing a green challenge indicates some measure of commitment to green strategy. For many smaller manufacturing enterprises, a commitment to green strategy, as defined by the public, may start with a top decision maker's proactive behavior toward a green issue or a signal from the market initiated by consumers or competitors leading to lower marketing performance. For others, awareness of direct punitive requirements promulgated by a regulatory authority stimulates top decision makers' attention.

Smaller manufacturing enterprises manage green issues differently than larger and more developed enterprises. For example, managers of smaller manufacturing enterprise are proactive toward green issue and fabricating products to clients' specifications, and so may not be able to alter the product specification under fabrication, but they can change the way the products are fabricated — in clean, well ventilated, lit conditions, using recycled water and nontoxic solvents.

Managers of smaller manufacturing enterprises who manage reactively perceive green challenges as managerial obstacles. Intermittently, they may make a commitment to green issues when market or competitive conditions require it, but feel they do not have the resources to implement their commitment consistently. Their tendencies are to acknowledge green challenges only when consumers, regulators, or even competitors compel them to do so. Such enterprises generally attempt to change or modify products and services marginally to be temporarily accepted as green products or services. Such enterprises frequently offer somewhat technologically or functionally obsolete products or services. They have only two future options — rescind the commitment to green initiatives or completely restructure. If the decision is to rescind commitment to green issues, future market potential is limited. For the enterprise to survive, the only viable option is to deploy marketing management and entirely restructure.

When initially confronted with green issues, larger manufacturing enterprises tend to initiate marketing and financial audits to determine the potential gains of responding to green challenges. When both audits are completed, management decides to what extent a commitment to green strategy should be made and how the entire enterprise needs to be repositioned in the market. Larger manufacturing enterprises may completely reorganize and even rewrite their mission to become totally committed to green marketing strategies. Some enterprises do not completely reorient to green issues even though the potential might be profitable; they adopt a more sequential strategy and may open a division, subsidiary, or enter a joint venture to make a full commitment to green marketing strategy over time.

Some managers of smaller manufacturing enterprises suggest that some domestically oriented managers cannot attain commitment to green issues due to insufficient resources. Consequently, they alter domestic marketing activities and market inferior products abroad. Such products are channeled into economically or technologically challenged markets. Internationally experienced managers point out that this short-term strategy usually results in an enterprise losing both markets — domestic and foreign. Some domestically oriented smaller manufacturing enterprises lose their commitment to green issues, leave domestic markets, and move abroad where markets or demand for specific products is not subject to green challenges. It is questionable what societal, technological, or marketing impacts such moves have on host markets.

3.4.2   *Green commitments to international markets*

Green strategy, as broadly perceived and defined by societies, is not the same in all markets. Various international markets respond differently to consumer demand for green products or services. In addition, government regulators may not address consumers' or users' concerns unless they become socially relevant. Lack of awareness or commitment to green issues in different markets present greater dilemmas for top decision makers of smaller manufacturing enterprises. Typically, the more technologically advanced and marketing proactive smaller manufacturing enterprises are managed by rational decision makers, the more likely it is that they will be committed to international green issues. This is particularly the case when entrepreneurs start ventures that have strong cross-border marketing potential. Such startup ventures do not differentiate among markets and modify products or services to meet the level of green demand in each market — domestic or international. They offer an array of green products or services in all markets equally even though a given market may not demand them.

Such an approach to green marketing initiatives contrasts with the marketing approach of smaller manufacturing enterprises that are more reserved and wait for an opportune occasion to introduce green products and services in foreign markets with incipient demand. The products or services subsequently marketed may be modifications of other green products or services available in other international markets. It is only when top decision makers fully commit to green issues that specific green products and services are developed and marketed for specific markets and subject to consumer demand and public approval. When green issues become significant, many entities separately or collectively must be involved with green issues; these include consumers and users, members of value chains, internal and external stakeholders, and investors. Only when social demand becomes socially relevant may legislative action follow. Although different entities may have varying degrees of commitment to green issues in international markets, collectively they arrive at an acceptable level resulting in compatible concerns over green issues in their individual markets.

3.5   Competitive Outlook and Market Posture

For top decision makers of smaller manufacturing enterprises making a commitment to green issues, it is important to understand how a broadly perceived or defined green strategy by the public impacts competitiveness and market posture. An enterprise needs to monitor its competitors regardless of whether it is domestically or internationally engaged. When an enterprise commits to green marketing strategies, it is influenced by its competitive outlook and market posture, although smaller manufacturing enterprises that benefit from strong markets and technological positions are less concerned about competition. Conversely, those with weak competitive positions need to be more aware of competitors' approaches to green issues. That is primarily why a commitment to green marketing initiatives depends on how committed the markets and competitors are.

A fundamental question concerning green marketing initiatives and public opinion is what is more important to an enterprise — responding to public demands for a broadly defined green strategy or responding to competitive market challenges? Managers suggest that proactive, technologically and marketing viable smaller manufacturing enterprises have high propensities to develop competitively strong market postures. As long as they market uniquely green products or services, their competitive positions will be secured; this further suggests that disadvantaged enterprises need to be conscious of their competition.

An interesting dilemma for smaller manufacturing enterprises with a strong commitment to green marketing initiatives is to decide if a line of green products or services may become the competitive factor in deciding their market posture, without considering the more general concerns over green strategy in the public domain? It appears that responses to such a dilemma are mixed. Most decision makers among smaller manufacturing enterprises agree that generally an unfavorable competitive outlook would take priority over any kind or level of public pressure concerning broadly defined green strategy.

Faced with such a dilemma, the main concern for managers of smaller manufacturing enterprises committed to green marketing strategies is how to define their commitment in the context of publicly defined green strategy and competitively driven green market postures? For some top decision makers of smaller internationally engaged manufacturing enterprises, the answer rests in the overall approaches in developing competitive green marketing strategies. Competitive green marketing strategies may range from a single integrated green marketing strategy uniformly applied across all markets to highly differentiated custom formulated green marketing strategies for each differentiated market. An increasing number of managers are making significant commitments to green concerns and formulating green marketing strategies to respond to green concerns on several levels of marketing initiatives — domestic and international.

Recommended Readings

1. Schnaars, S. P. (1991). *Marketing Strategy: A Customer-Driven Approach* (The Free Press, New York, NY).
2. Tesar, G., Moini, H., Kuada, J. and Sørensen, O. J. (2010). *Smaller Manufacturing Enterprises in an International Context: A Longitudinal Exploration* (Imperial College Press, London, UK).

Chapter 4

Marketing Strategies for Green Issues

Marketing strategy, in the context of smaller manufacturing enterprises, is defined as a managerial philosophy within which managers intend to realize marketing objectives. More specifically, marketing strategy is a series of interrelated decisions about target consumers, market segments, and target markets combined with a coordinated mix of marketing variables subject to optimal allocation of available resources. There is a direct connection between the missions and the marketing strategies they deploy among consumer-oriented smaller manufacturing enterprises. This approach to marketing management suggests that the mission of each enterprise provides an intellectual space for a unique marketing philosophy. The managerial philosophy of the individual enterprise results in marketing strategies formulated to successfully market products and services and compete.

4.1 Marketing Strategy

Marketing managers, including some among smaller manufacturing enterprises, define marketing strategy as a system of interactive marketing variables needed to facilitate the flow of products and services to consumers. The fundamental assumption is that consumers are the focal points of all marketing activities and are sources of information for marketing products and services. Most marketing managers managing entrepreneurial startups, especially high-technology products or services, point out that marketing strategy consists of variables needed to direct marketing initiatives from entrepreneurial discoveries to their implementation. The assumption behind this approach is that entrepreneurs often develop products or services for which there is no active demand; it is up to the entrepreneurs to stimulate demand. This definition of marketing strategy implies demand stimulation or creation. The two concepts of marketing strategy are similar except that the first assumes that marketing strategies are based on information gathered from consumers, while the second assumes that entrepreneurs have sufficient information to make marketing decisions without consumer input. The first approach is known as market pull, while the second is known as market push in marketing.

A more practical view of marketing strategy perceives it as a system of interrelated factors directing marketing initiatives from entrepreneurial discoveries of marketing opportunities to their implementation among consumers in competitive markets. Marketing opportunities are expressed in terms of product or service ideas, concepts, prototypes, and products. Marketing strategies are formulated for specific products intended to be marketed in defined market segments where consumer profiles are matched directly with product or service attributes.

Information gathered from marketing research tempered by the marketing and technological abilities of an enterprise as defined by its mission is required to establish the precise relationship between product or service attributes and the consumer profiles contained in a market segment. Then, potential marketing opportunities verified through marketing research studies can be matched against consumers' demand and behavior. Market segments are constructed based on potential consumer demand estimated by examining cohorts of consumers and products or services with attributes that match the attributes sought by the consumer cohorts. Decisions are made concerning the external environment forces shaping the market and the enterprise based on the exact nature of these relationships. The impact of external environmental forces will be minimal if initial relationships between products and services and the target market segment have been accurately and strategically defined. The market will not accept the products or services if they have not been defined within the relevant external environment, such as economic, legal, and social factors, or even lifestyles.

Relationships between market segments and products or services are limited by the available resources needed to market them. A marketing strategy must be accompanied by a budget for it. Budgets intended for a marketing strategy, especially among smaller manufacturing enterprises, are, at best, estimates. The budget might be optimistic or pessimistic depending on managers' ability to identify and assess the impact a product or a service will have on a market. Managers of low-technology, smaller manufacturing enterprise tend to underestimate costs involved in introducing products or services in a market segment while managers of high-technology enterprises tend to overestimate costs. Marketing strategies are often assigned budgets with provisions for over-runs or under-runs with specified limits.

A marketing strategy must recognize competition. Managers must define what products or services, and more importantly, with what entities they compete when formulating a marketing strategy. The character of the competition must be specified and serve as a constraint. Enterprises may compete on a product-by-product or service-by-service basis without taking into consideration a competitor's financial strength. Managers of smaller manufacturing enterprises often perceive competitors at this minimal level. Understanding competitor's marketing and technological competencies is the other extreme of perceiving competitors. Some managers of high-technology startups suggest that they have an advantage of in developing marketing strategies for unique markets and have no competitors. Other managers point out that they can identify and select entities with which they want to compete for consumer demand.

The core features of a marketing strategy are controllable variables interpreted as either the four marketing variables: product, price, promotion, and place; or their variants — product and service, communication, and distribution mixes. Managers of smaller manufacturing enterprises often suggest that the latter are more suited for their marketing initiatives and strategy formation as their personal marketing management philosophy evolves. The notion of marketing mixes is more flexible; it might be better suited for formulating marketing strategies for Internet marketing.

In this framework, the product or service as a component of marketing strategy is perceived as both a fixed and flexible variable. It is fixed in the sense that the product or service has been developed based on distinct specifications derived from a clearly identified and selected market segment consisting of preferred consumers. Products and services have unique sets of physical, functional, and psychological attributes which connect the product with its customers (by definition, services do not have a set of physical attributes). Both physical and psychological attributes can be altered by fine-tuning the products or services to better serve customers. A product can be altered by substituting different materials, offering color options, or making the product quieter.

The promotional mix informs consumers via various communication channels such as the Internet, social media, or direct advertising. These channels can be modified in response to changing market conditions by adjusting the message or responding to changing environmental conditions. High-technology products that require long training periods with a steep learning curve often pre-advertise the fact that the product may have a significant impact on consumers' everyday lives. Modern smart telephones combine several functions such as cameras, note taking, and diaries among others that users need to learn how to use. A promotional mix serves an important purpose in informing users how the product will change their everyday habits.

The distribution mix adjusts how a product or service reaches intended consumers. The overall objective of a distribution mix is to formulate an optimal channel through which a product will connect with consumers. A distribution mix is intended to provide time, place, and possession utility — a product needs to arrive on time at a specified address and safely into the hands of consumers. This is particularly important in the Internet age. Consumers also need the ability to conveniently and efficiently return a product if they are not satisfied with it. Any optimal channel is subject to adjustments over time. The movement from location-based shopping to Internet shopping is a good example of how a distribution mix designed for a conventional product may dramatically change over time because of evolving technology.

The variables that are the core of a marketing strategy also interact with each other. Improvements in protective packaging may change how a product is shipped or displayed. For example, making the size of a package smaller without changing the weight of the content may save on shipping and decrease shelf space in a grocery store. Using more durable recycled package material may convey a message suggesting environmental awareness. Internet marketing presents additional challenges in formulating marketing strategies. Distribution methods for products purchased via the Internet require additional facilities and arrangements with outside shipping services. Consumers need to return unwanted merchandise and to understand relevant return policies. Addressing policy issues may be part of a promotional effort. Differentiated pricing and price promotion may have a significant impact on where the product will be purchased — in a retail store or over the Internet. These variables, within a marketing strategy, determine how products and services are placed in the market and how they are positioned competitively.

The above factors provide the conceptual foundation for an optimal marketing strategy. Managers of smaller manufacturing enterprises need to build on this foundation and realize that marketing strategies respond to two sets of needs — those defined by consumers and those specified by society as reflected in outside environmental conditions. It is up to decision makers responsible for marketing initiatives and strategies to adjust them accordingly. Adjustments may be challenging for some smaller manufacturing enterprises, because they might change the way an enterprise operates and, potentially, some changes might be financially demanding. Nevertheless, a marketing strategy must be flexible and responsive to market challenges and environmental constraints.

4.2   Marketing Strategy and Innovation

In consumer-oriented markets, unique managerial philosophies guide formation of marketing strategies and determine the amount and nature of innovation necessary to implement them. An innovation necessary to implement a marketing strategy is determined by the availability of resources. High technology enterprises that enter a market with technologically innovative products or services decide what impact their innovation will have and formulate marketing strategies accordingly. It is more difficult to judge what level of technological innovation to deploy in the market as enterprises move lower on the scale of achievable innovation. Some managers prefer to introduce new marketing approaches or reposition products or services and refer to such changes as marketing innovation.

Many smaller manufacturing enterprises contemplate a tradeoff between technological and marketing innovation when faced with such decisions. Technological innovation results from an enterprise's ability to find new ways to solve complex technical problems, deploy new engineering approaches to solve problems based on old methods or conventions, or anticipate future problems not possible to solve with old or existing scientific knowledge. However, new technological solutions to current problems, introduced by smaller manufacturing enterprises in consumer markets, cannot be considered an innovation unless consumers have accepted the solution to current problems. If consumers reject a technologically new product or service, for whatever reason, it is not an innovation. For example, if a technologically new product is perceived by consumers as too complex and requires long learning curve, consumers may reject it. It will not be considered an innovation by the rest of the market even if a small number of consumers accept the product as a novelty.

Marketing innovation relates to how products and services are marketed. Minor innovative changes in an entire value chain may lead to a marketing innovation. Changes in product or service design, manufacturing processes, or adjustments in marketing strategies may potentially trigger marketing innovation. For example, repackaging a product for easier use — dispensing a product such as detergent more economically in a washing application — if accepted by a significant number of consumers, may be considered a marketing innovation. An alteration in a product's promotional campaign from mass directed efforts to highly personalized approaches may be accepted as an important marketing innovation by managers and consumers.

Marketing strategies and marketing innovation require a delicate balance of relationships among managerial philosophies, marketing strategies, and innovative activities. Top decision makers must recognize these concepts; carefully balance them for all marketing initiatives. Top decision makers need to communicate their decisions to all levels of management. Top decision makers also need to be cognizant of these relationships and balances when responding to changing market demand or when an enterprise confronts major technological or market discontinuities and competition. Such conditions may require complete reexamination of its survival in some instance.

Smaller manufacturing enterprises managed by craftsmen-type managers approach the above conditions and resulting challenges from a personal, and often somewhat dictatorial, attitude. The dynamics of their personal managerial philosophy, marketing strategy, and innovation are not generally communicated and available to others. The balance between types of innovation often are not clear to craftsman-type managers because of their intense focus on making a product or offering a service. Smaller manufacturing enterprise managers with promotional tendencies may specify some of the relationships and define the balance between the types of innovation, but only on as needed basis in response to changing market demand or competitive market position. Rational-type managers, particularly those responsible for technology-based smaller manufacturing enterprises, are more likely to specify the relationship among their managerial philosophies and balance their innovation and marketing strategies.

The marketing strategy is one of the cornerstones of marketing management along with managerial philosophy and innovation. The control factor in formulating a marketing strategy is the ability of a smaller manufacturing enterprise to balance technological and marketing innovations. The resulting balance between the two is imbedded in innovative products and services. That is, each product or service is an integral part of a marketing strategy exclusively formulated for the product or service and based on a strategically specified level of technological and marketing innovation.

4.3   Context of Green Marketing Strategies

Green marketing strategies among smaller manufacturing enterprises do not differ much from conventional marketing strategies. Most managers of smaller manufacturing enterprises consider the notion of green as an added dimension to conventional marketing strategies. What a green factor represents in green marketing strategies is somewhat arbitrary for such managers. Other managers consider the notion of green a component of a new marketing management philosophy.

Enterprises primarily interested in allocating and optimizing resources tend to consider green issues as new dimensions added to an enterprise's managerial philosophy that may potentially force the enterprise to redefine its mission. For example, a traditional farm growing genetically modified corn for human consumption may redefine its mission and become a grower of organic corn using organic fertilizer and the latest farming methods. On the opposite end of the scale, managers challenged with resource shortages and with a subjective personal managerial philosophy tend to judge green issues as product or service attributes that, if necessary, can be added at some point to the value creation chain. They believe that products or services can be redesigned or otherwise modified. These managers also suggest that green dimensions can be achieved by adjusting marketing activities such as promotional activities, redesigning packaging, or altering ingredients. For example, a manufacturer of interior paints may promote products as green by replacing chemicals that have a strong industrial odor with a less offensive ingredient. The key decision is how green issues become part of green marketing strategies regardless of how green issues are perceived by managers of smaller manufacturing enterprises?

Smaller manufacturing enterprises require innovative thinking to formulate and implement green marketing strategies. Innovative thinking and green marketing initiatives are interconnected and become parts of managers' overall green managerial philosophies. Based on marketing orientation, green managerial philosophies define levels of commitment by an enterprise to green issues and specify innovations needed to successfully implement green marketing initiatives. The management of each smaller manufacturing enterprise needs to decide what level of resources they are willing to commit to green issues, since a commitment to green issues varies significantly.

Commitment to green issues may be reached on several levels in a small manufacturing enterprise. If an enterprise makes a total commitment to green issues, redefines its mission, and defines a new green managerial philosophy, the entire enterprise assumes new green marketing goals and objectives. This implies that its products and services will be, by definition, green. All marketing activities, starting with allocating resources, managing productive activities, operating logistical systems, and designing communication channels will have green components.

Innovative thinking begins with ideas that contribute to the realization of green products and services. For some smaller manufacturing enterprises, this includes the transformation of administrative and manufacturing facilities to green facilities, such as converting to solar heating, generating solar or wind energy, recycling water used for production purposes, moving toward paperless offices. As efforts to be green enter the managerial and physical levels of an enterprise, every function is, to some degree, assimilated and eventually integrated into the overall green commitment of the enterprise.

Commitment to green issues on functional levels among smaller manufacturing enterprises is implemented through each function. Since some smaller manufacturing enterprises tend to combine functions such as product design, development, and engineering, it becomes easier to implement green issues. In more complex enterprises, each function focuses on its core activities and interprets green issues in the framework of its function. For example, the marketing research function will collect information from consumers; identify consumers' green perception, preferences, and attitudes;

generate information relevant to product development, including specification for potential products or services and their expected attributes, among other packets of information. Another example is when sales specialists gather information about consumers' buying behavior and about how consumers evaluate the role of green issues as related to the entire sales process. Engineering develops more efficient manufacturing lines with smaller carbon footprints. All activities leading to improvements in green performance by individual functions contribute to the overall green commitment and may contribute to more credible green marketing strategies.

In some cases, functions perform specific tasks and are responsible for performing those tasks under green conditions. For example, product design, development, and engineering may be in environmentally green remotely located facilities that contribute to the green reputation of the products. Engineering facilities may be placed next to production so that any mechanical or quality control problems are resolved quickly. Engineers may also be charged with identifying nonpolluting materials and making products or services functionally more efficient and useable. Finished inventory may be housed in dark, controlled environments, equipped with automation systems. Such efforts to gravitate toward green conditions vary from one enterprise to another, and require innovative thinking and managerial philosophies that stimulate a strong green focus among all functions.

The basic level on which a commitment to green issues can be demonstrated by smaller manufacturing enterprises is on the level of their products or services. An entire enterprise and its infrastructure can focus on producing a green product or offering a green service. Green products and services represent the level of commitment to green issues and project the green image of the entire enterprise. All attributes of a product or service can be expressed as green or presented as having the appearance of being green. Managers responsible for marketing activities among less market-oriented smaller manufacturing enterprises point out that the simple appearance of being green is sufficient in some markets. It is not sufficient in more-advanced markets, especially for products or services with high technology content. Consumers easily discern the nature of real commitment to green issues.

Smaller manufacturing enterprises generally demonstrate commitment to green issues both internally and externally. Internally, commitment to green issues is spread throughout organizational hierarchies, managerial functions, and individual operations. An internal commitment to green issues is demonstrated by the green physical appearance of facilities, green attitudes and convictions of managers and employees, and green attitudes toward all stakeholders. Externally, smaller manufacturing enterprises tend to communicate commitment to green issues though green products or services, mostly to customers. Often the commitment to green issues is not communicated well with the public, regulators, and even some customers. Managers familiar with green issues suggest that internal and external communication concerning green issues must be combined. Consumers want to understand the entire scope of marketing activities related to their consumption of green products or services.

4.4   Framework for Green Marketing Strategy

A green marketing strategy is formulated to market a product or service designed, developed, and produced specifically to address a commitment made by a smaller manufacturing enterprise in response to green consumer demand. Each green marketing strategy is unique and characteristic of the level of commitment made by an enterprise to green issues. It represents a marketing channel that delivers green value to consumers who seek green consumption options. Consumers expect that an enterprise that commits to function as a green enterprise will deliver products or services that complement green consumers in their consumption and post-consumption experiences and will satisfy their lifestyles.

In the opinion of managers of smaller manufacturing enterprises, green marketing strategies close the connections between green commitments they make to green issues and consumers who include green products or services in their consumption processes because they feel obligated to protect and preserve the natural environment around them. Commitment to green issues is a social contract between green producers and consumers. It is important to realize that it is in this framework that green marketing strategies must be formulated. It is equally important to understand that green marketing strategies are the tools of the managers who formulate them.

Managers of smaller manufacturing enterprises must understand consumer behavior, especially what motivates consumers to demand green products or services in order to formulate green marketing strategies. Marketing research needs to be conducted to understand consumers' motivations for purchasing green products or services. Consumers' perceptions of products and services, which trigger preferences for green products and services, form attitudes toward them. To a limited degree, three components of consumer behavior — perceptions, preferences, and attitudes — stimulate needs and wants that generate demand for green products or services.

4.4.1 *Consumer behavior*

The consumption behavior reflected in consumers' lifestyles often indicates why consumers want green products or services. Social and environmental events around consumers' influence their lifestyles. If they organize their lifestyles with a strong affinity to protect the environment, they will structure their consumption accordingly. Marketing managers need to understand this process and market appropriate green products and services to satisfy green consumer demand.

Green consumers are aware of what products or services they need to satisfy their lifestyles. They gather information from various sources — family, relatives, coworkers, and friends — in their personal networks. A personal social network becomes an important reference group for green consumers. They typically verify information on the Internet. Green consumers search for products or services they consider suitable; compare them to other available options; select the best option; and decide on the economic, social, and psychological value of a product or service. The decision to buy or not to buy is also dependent on the price of the product or service, place of purchase such as a retail establishment or the Internet, and timing of delivery.

Smaller green manufacturing enterprises develop green products and services to satisfy market demand as expressed by consumption requirements of green consumers. These connections serve as frameworks for formulating green marketing strategies. A green marketing strategy must be formulated to link specifically developed green products or services with consumption preferences and lifestyles of individual consumers. However, green consumers do not behave as single individuals; they behave similarly and form groups or market segments with similar lifestyles that in turn, are parts of larger consumer markets. Consumers have distinctive lifestyles. Market segments are comprised of consumers with similar lifestyles and segments with similar lifestyles add up to markets for green products and services. The green products or services consumed by individual consumers represent a common denominator among them.

4.4.2 *Post-consumption*

What happens to green products or services at the end of their usefulness is important in the lifestyles of green consumers today. This is a challenge for many green consumers. Some nondurable green products are simply used up — food items, laundry detergents, agricultural products. However, there are residual remains such as packaging. What options are available to recycle the residuals? Green consumers today expect that packaging is recyclable either throughout a local municipality or by returning it to the source of origin — the manufacturer.

More durable products with long-lasting economic, social, or psychological value are more difficult to accommodate in post-consumption among green consumers. An increasing number of green consumers advocate that producers of durable products, including smaller manufacturing enterprises, must provide a system of recycling or otherwise disposing of product residuals in a way that does not harm the physical environment or deplete nonrenewable resources. Some managers responsible for green issues among smaller manufacturing enterprises suggest that facilities designed to accommodate product residuals could be shared or might be developed as communal facilities. The notion of shared facilities has limited acceptance by green consumers who feel that the overall life of a product spans from its conception to a post-consumption point where a durable product does not have any intrinsic value for its original consumer but is still the responsibility of the original manufacturer.

Green consumers believe that durable products such as home appliances or mechanical equipment used around the house not only have several value levels and can be remarketed to other green consumers but they also have a final material recyclable value. Thus, manufacturers of durable products may be responsible for secondary markets for their products and their terminal scrap value. For example, the owner of an older version of a fully functional electric lawn mower with a long electric cord may replace it with a newer rechargeable lawn mower because of owner's psychological preferences. The owner of the original lawn mower expects that the previous lawn mower will be resold or recycled and the residual material reused in some appropriate form. Such expectations by green consumers are presented without any social or personal cost considerations that for some smaller manufacturing enterprises present another challenge — a pricing dilemma. How should the value of a product be determined?

4.5   Green Marketing Strategies

Green marketing strategies begin with green products or services offered to green consumers. The green products or services have specified green attributes based on information generated from green consumers through marketing and scientific research, including consumer behavior studies, market dynamics, and competitive intelligence. Product or service attributes are defined, tested, and integrated into the entire marketing process. They are compared to originally define green consumer profiles, the characteristics of market segments, and combined into markets for an accurate match between products and services offerings and demands of green consumers. An effective and efficient green marketing strategy is formulated to optimize this relationship. However, such relationships in dynamic situations with fluctuations in market supply and demand for green products or services may need adjustment. Such adjustments are made by altering controllable variables in the marketing mix when necessary. Most managers of smaller manufacturing enterprises perceive the product, promotion, price, and place as the traditional marketing variables.

4.5.1 *Product or service adjustments*

Product adjustments in a green marketing strategy can be made by changing the makeup of each set of attributes — functional, physical, and psychological. The green functional attributes are most difficult to adjust because a product or a service is intended for specific applications defined by consumers. Some green functional capabilities may be added or removed, but any changes in green functional performance of a product or service needs to be verified by consumers. The latitude for adjustment of physical attributes is greater with innovative thinking. Physical components of products assumed to be green made from nonrecyclable materials may be replaced with recyclable materials. Green products can be made to weigh less, use less energy, or be more ergonomic. Even the colors of products may impact how the physical attributes of green products are perceived.

The psychological attributes of green products can respond quickly to necessary market or competitive changes when implementing a green marketing strategy. Psychological attributes are closely aligned with consumers' perceptions, preferences, and attitudes which factor into their behavior. A green product may be perceived positively under some conditions in a consumption process and negatively under others. For example, a green product can be favorably accepted by green consumers when the necessary infrastructure for a product is in place, but negatively when the infrastructure is only marginal or does not exist at all — such is the case of electric cars as infrastructural deficiencies slow their diffusion. Preferences for green products may vary because of perceived differences in how green a product or service is. Green consumers prefer rechargeable electric lawn mowers to the ones powered by gasoline. Attitudes toward green products or services may change dramatically depending on if they are in product adoption mode or in the diffusion of innovation cycle. Green consumers change attitudes toward products quickly and mostly because of psychological attributes.

4.5.2 *Pricing adjustments*

Pricing adjustments of green products or services require innovative insight into the behavior of green consumers. Price information availability for green products or services is immense; green consumers have access to price information on many levels of marketing. They can do comparative price shopping in retail locations by simply using their smart telephones to scan green product information and receive instant feedback on pricing information from competitors in the surrounding retail area. Retailers of durable goods such as automobiles, appliances, or electronics frequently let consumers compare prices on their own computers by using competitive profile software or posting competitors daily prices. Online connectivity and the Internet provide additional opportunities for green consumers to compare prices before they decide on the level of shopping convenience they need and how much they are willing to pay.

The technological developments, marketing approaches by competitors, and behavioral aspects of green consumers pose major challenges for smaller manufacturing enterprises and their managers in adjusting green marketing strategy from a pricing perspective. It is important to note that some green consumers initially perceive green product or services as higher priced than conventional counterparts. It is difficult for managers to price either tangible or intangible green products or service components under these conditions. For example, pricing an environmentally safe material higher is difficult if it does not improve green performance; green consumers are more likely to accept a price increase if it does. The same situation exists with intangible green components that are sometimes labeled as created or assumed components. Just because a green product is defined in promotional or advertising campaigns as "green engineered and manufactured under environmental standards", it may be perceived differently by individual green consumers and does not merit a price increase.

Managers among leading smaller green manufacturing enterprises indicate that each component, ingredient, or part of a green product or service must be priced separately. In addition, a specific value may be determined for each manual or automated operation in the manufacturing, fabrication, or delivery of green products or services. Some manually crafted or fabricated green products may be valued more than those produced on automated production lines. Examples can be found in the manufacturing and retailing of consumer products such as custom built furniture from recycled material, organically grown agricultural products, or textiles produced from recycled materials — all may be valued more than versions manufactured or produced on automated systems. It is important to understand how tangible and intangible factors help determine the value and thus, the price for green consumers. How much are green consumers are willing to pay for various attributes of green products or services?

4.5.3   *Promotional adjustments*

Promotion as a controllable variable consists of advertising, sales promotion, packaging, and public relations for smaller manufacturing enterprises. Marketing specialists among smaller manufacturing enterprises communicate with green consumers through several channels. Traditional print-based communication channels reach large audiences, but the Internet and social media based-communication systems are close behind.

Communication messages needs to be adjusted frequently to accommodate market changes or competitive pressures. Communication with green consumers is changing and moving from mass print media to directed and personal telecommunication-based media due to the rapid evolution of communication technology. Print media is the slowest and least responsive; it takes time to change the message and place it in print media such as newspapers, magazines, or trade publications. Television or radio advertising is flexible and effective for some products or services, especially in urban areas where the audience base is strong and well established. However, telecommunication-based social media delivers a message fastest.

Electronic-based social media has the flexibility to communicate a targeted message quickly by reaching large numbers of green consumers at almost any time of the day and anywhere in the market. It also has an added dimension — green consumers can communicate with each other instantly over the same media, present their opinions as to whether they like or dislike a particular green product of service, or simply comment on the message itself.

Most smaller manufacturing enterprises maintain an Internet webpage which communicates directly with customers or consumers and the public. Webpage-based communications respond quickly to necessary adjustments in information messaging and can generate fast positive or negative feedback. However, social media communication is more directed and generates even faster responses. Social media-based messages are frequently accompanied by electronically forwarded printable incentives such as personalized coupons or invitations to private sales events. Today, managers of smaller manufacturing enterprises use electronically printable media to keep green consumers interested and informed. Similar approaches are used to communicate with suppliers, distributors, investors, and other entities in or outside value chains.

Packaging plays an important role in promoting green products or services — packaging is a part of the overall image green consumers expect. Green consumers expect food products to be in recycled packaging, merchandise delivered to homes to use in containers made from recycled materials, and even the ink used to print advertising on containers to be environmentally safe. The recent surge in package and container design and engineering to minimize the use of recycled packaging material, assumed to be safe and durable, is a direct response to increased shipments of merchandise ordered via the Internet. It is economically feasible for some smaller manufacturing enterprises which market green products to integrate the design and engineering of package and shipment containers at the same time as they develop a new green product and ready it for distribution.

Public relations among smaller manufacturing enterprises are more important as demand for green products and services grow. Managers realize the need to communicate with the public as much as with green consumers. Green consumers communicate not only among themselves but also serve as innovators or early adopters who advocate for green products and services to the public. Green consumers contribute to stimulating green demand by using green products and services.

Managers need to present viable and credible images for their enterprises by participating in community action, improving the local physical environment, conserving resources, or presenting a visible presence in public green initiatives. For example, reducing pollution, installing solar panels or wind turbines, or recycling material such as steel or plastics used in production is important in presenting a green public image. Conducting factory tours to demonstrate how green products are produced, warehoused, and transported increases green credibility among the public.

4.5.4 *Place adjustments*

Place as a controllable variable in a marketing mix represents by what means product or services are delivered to consumers — including finished inventory, warehousing, physical handling, transportation, and other necessary mechanical or automated processes needed to move products from production to consumption. This important process for green products or services needs to be systematically monitored as it is closely related to the overall green image of an enterprise. Smaller manufacturing enterprises may participate, out of necessity, in supply chains, to secure supplies they need. It is important to consider that membership in a substandard supply chain may have a devastating impact on the green image of an enterprise. Green products or services must be available to green consumers through green distribution channels. Marketing managers of green enterprises need to seek compatible supply and distribution chains to manage their green image.

Managers of smaller green manufacturing enterprises implicate that a place variable is perhaps the most problematic for green products or services to specify and the most difficult to adjust due to several factors. Many supply chains are not environmentally sound, may have not subscribed to environmental standards in the quality of supplies they provide, or may have questionable sources. Intermediate resellers may not track where original supplies originate and simply pass them on. Smaller manufacturing enterprises committed to green issues need to participate in supply chains consistent with their own levels of green commitment. The same concerns apply to distribution chains. Green products and services pass through them, and thus entire distribution channels must present a green image as extensions of green enterprises. The physical handling of components must be consistent with the overall green image of an enterprise.

Safety is an important aspect of handling green products and services. Green consumers are concerned with the safety and contamination of green products and services. If a product is promoted as green and its safety and purity is compromised during distribution, green consumers will be reluctant to purchase it. For example, herbal tea grown under organic conditions, sun dried, and hand packaged must have green protective packaging and flow through a green distribution channel safely without extreme temperature fluctuation, damaged packaging, or other contamination. Distribution channels must be designed as green before any green products flow through them.

Efforts to distribute green products may be even more complex due to the rapidly changing distribution technology connected with the Internet. The increasing number of products purchased via the Internet and the shortening of shipping time to green consumers, places pressure on various modes of delivery. Intermediaries responsible for fast deliveries are introducing alternative technologies to deliver products as effectively and efficiently as possible. This sometimes requires subcontracting specialized deliveries to smaller agencies. Green consumers expect that all types of delivery services of green products or services meet the same level of expectations.

Retailing services are also changing, due to increasing Internet shopping habits of green consumer, and demand adjustments in how green products are delivered. Most retailers offer alternative ways to shop. Computer ordering facilities are available in stores, retail stores accept returns of unwanted merchandise, and retail personnel are instructed to assist ordering on the computer in the store if the merchandise is not in the store. Green products need to fit into the overall distribution channel, but need to be differentiated from similar products that are not green. Marketing managers among smaller green manufacturing enterprises constantly assess how green products or services need to be integrated into both the Internet shopping environment and retailing practices since both change rapidly.

4.6 Environmental Conditions and Green Marketing Strategy

Formulating green marketing strategies can be constrained by the environmental conditions around smaller manufacturing enterprises. Environmental forces can directly impact their green initiatives and green marketing strategies. Environmental forces such as changing social conditions driving green issues, fluctuating economic conditions, rapid diffusion of new technology, and evolving consumers' lifestyles — especially lifestyles of green consumers, must be closely monitored and their impact directly related to changes in green marketing strategy.

Social conditions or forces that drive green issues need to be continuously monitored because they may be detrimental to green products and services and their market dynamics. For example, a changing political climate may influence to what extent politicians will continue to commit to green issues if their commitment will intensify whereby demand for green products or services may increase. Regulatory guidelines demanded by green consumers may change simply due to an industrial accident or natural disaster. Given the connection between a political climate and regulatory oversight, it is difficult for managers to predict how their green products or services might be affected by changes in the political climate.

Diffusion of new technology in green markets needs to be monitored because it tends to gradually erode the traditional bases of green products. As an example, fishing industries that fished in ocean waters are making a technological shift to farm grow fish and distribute them as more environmentally friendly products. Technological forces impact the green lifestyles of consumers. The introduction of electric automobiles is changing the driving habits of green consumers. Availability of solar panels for home use is decreasing reliance on public and private utilities; they, in turn, may have to think about green consumers differently, perhaps as co-producers of energy rather than customers.

Environmental conditions impact the green marketing strategies of smaller manufacturing enterprises. As such conditions change, managers are typically challenged to adjust the marketing variables that make up their green marketing strategies. Changes need to be made quickly and effectively so they do not disturb fundamental relationships between green products and services and the green consumers who generate market demand for green products and services.

Competition may significantly impact implementation of green marketing strategy. Some marketing managers among high-technology, smaller green manufacturing enterprises suggest they can select the competitors with whom they are willing to compete, not all smaller green manufacturing enterprises experience similar competitive conditions. Competitors change quickly; some enter critical markets, and others leave the same markets. Competitive dynamics in the market result from changes in economic conditions and consumer dynamics, rapid diffusion of new technology, or consumer preferences among others.

Marketing green products or services is a complex and highly dynamic process. Competitive dynamics in green markets stem from factors that are difficult to determine initially. Slight adjustments of consumer prices for products that are essential to consumers' lifestyles, such as the cost of commuting to work may significantly reduce the purchase of green products considered to be marginally supportive of certain aspects of consumers' green lifestyles. There are many examples of competition among green products or services. For example, a green product designed, developed, manufactured, and distributed as a green product under sound environmental conditions may be faced by a competitor with a marginally green product marketed and distributed through questionable retailing channels. Managers must be able to clearly differentiate such products and adjust their green marketing strategy to maintain their green customers.

The budget that top decision makers among smaller manufacturing enterprises set for each green marketing strategy is the final factor that determines the nature of a green marketing strategy. Marketing managers propose budgets needed to implement marketing strategies, but consider budgets as one of the noncontrollable variables in marketing initiatives, including marketing strategies since they do not have the full control over budgets. Budgets set especially for green marketing strategies need to be flexible and to anticipate, within margins, any potential adjustments required to reach green consumers, face changing environmental conditions, and remain competitive.

Recommended Readings

1. Kotler, P. and Armstrong, G. (2016). *Principles of Marketing*, Global Edition (Pearson Education Limited, Essex, UK).
2. Schnaars, S. P. (1991). *Marketing Strategy: A Customer-Driven Approach* (The Free Press, New York, NY).
3. Tesar, G., Moini, H., Kuada, J. and Sørensen, O. J. (2010). *Smaller Manufacturing Enterprises in an International Context: A Longitudinal Exploration* (Imperial College Press, London, UK).

Chapter 5

Financial Analysis of Green Projects

A commitment to green marketing strategies could have significant financial implications. Small manufacturing enterprises must devise a financial strategy that is coherent with their green marketing strategies. While some enterprises consider simple modification of their product as adoption of a green marketing strategy, others may design new products that require significant investments in equipment and buildings. Even a simple modification in a product may require investment in machinery or equipment. Therefore, enterprises must decide if their project adds any value to their firms or not. Otherwise, it might be better to invest in other projects. Furthermore, enterprises might prefer a project because it achieves other nonfinancial objectives. Although financial evaluations offer results that can be used to compare different projects, it is the job of the managers to decide which project to choose. The important questions are how these enterprises assess which project is worthy of their investments and how to get the needed capital for them. This chapter will address these questions.

5.1 Management Commitment to Green Marketing Strategies

Assimilating "green" strategy into marketing strategies is a multifaceted and demanding process. Increasingly, consumers are becoming more conscientious of the need for sustainability and environmental protection that has resulted in a shift in management mindsets from reactive to proactive management. Managers have learned that by practicing a proactive green strategy such as changing the nature of their products or services they could gain a competitive advantage. Additionally, enterprises could reduce costs and improve the quality of their products, open new markets, and improve their corporate image, for possible positive long-term effects on their financial performance. Despite all these benefits, it has to be acknowledged that the implementation of "green" strategies may also raises a number of issues for enterprises regarding the alignment of their new strategic activities with existing ones, the range and uniformity of changes across enterprise divisions, and the pace of the strategic changes.

The purpose of any green enterprise is to further social and ethical standards. Before implementing a new business strategy, enterprise managers must consider the interests of their constituencies, including stockholders. Financial decisions with respect to investment in green projects must create competitive advantages that would allow enterprises to achieve a viable financial performance. For any green strategy to succeed, a strong commitment by top managers is a necessity.

5.2   Green Marketing Strategy and the Enterprise Performance

Green marketing strategies play an important role in an enterprise's success. They link industrial ecological concerns with environmental sustainability, as part of the overall corporate green strategy. Since green marketing strategies impact enterprises in a number of ways, an enterprise must examine all aspects of its marketing mix such as price, product, communication, and distribution.

Green marketing strategies affect an enterprise's pricing of products or services. Installing new machinery, equipment, and other related expenses could be substantial. However, reducing wasteful packaging materials could also reduce some of the costs of going green. This is important especially when packaging costs for some products comprise a large part of production costs. Additional promotional costs to advertise new or improved eco-conscious products can raise unit costs. Obviously, these extra costs are pooled into the cost of production leading to a higher price for the customers.

There are environmentally conscious consumers who actively seek to purchase only organic or eco-friendly goods and services, whereas many still consider these products and services to be a premium that they are willing to purchase only occasionally. In addition, competition may force some enterprises, especially smaller ones, to keep prices low. This is also true when customers' price elasticity is high which prevents enterprises from raising their prices. It is imperative for enterprises to justify their actions through persuasive advertising and communication or introduction of a green product may not be financially feasible.

Adopting green marketing strategies impacts an enterprise's products and services. Generally, a product is called "green" when its manufacturing process is less harmful to the environment. Some enterprises consider a simple change in packaging or labeling their products as adoption of green strategy. Others may decide to revamp the manufacturing process in order to build a green product.

The success of green marketing strategies also depends on how enterprises connect with stakeholders by informing them about their green products and services. Enterprises have numerous ways to communicate with customers about their green commitments, efforts and achievements. Public relation is one way to justify a green strategy. Enterprises can also use advertising to communicate the benefits of green products and explain features and prices of their products.

Green marketing strategies can also affect the distribution of products and services by improving an enterprise's performance. As larger numbers of customers choose green products and services, enterprises must select a distribution channel that minimizes the ecological impacts of their products. Product transportation is responsible for most of the damage to the environment. Implementing safety precautions during transportation of products is very critical. Increased in safety in delivery of products can directly affect cost of production and indirectly the enterprise's profitability.

Enterprises can transform their distribution chains to become more environmentally friendly in three ways: (1) Shrink size or reduce materials used in packaging to reduce distribution costs for smaller packaging and minimize damage to the environment by using fewer hazardous materials. However, the distribution costs can also increase if the new packaging requires more expensive materials. (2) Develop reusable products, ensuring that customers can return recyclable materials to the enterprise or to recycling partners who have agreed to receive recyclable products at a cost to enterprises. This will increase distribution costs. (3) Enterprises can also require suppliers to meet certain environmental standards. This may also increase the cost of production as suppliers may demand a higher price.

It is a necessity for managers to understand the financial significances of these decisions. Can enterprises add in the additional costs into prices or they must absorb these costs, at the expense of shareholders? An enterprise must have a better understanding of its customers' desires and thought processes in order to have better and more effective green marketing strategies. Green marketing strategies can increase an enterprise's competitive advantage by improving customer loyalty leading to larger market share, but each enterprise must analyze and choose the best marketing strategies that fit its values and customers' expectations. These issues are more critical for smaller manufacturing enterprises.

5.3   Green Strategy and Financial Performance

Numerous studies have examined the impact of green strategy on an enterprise's financial performance. Their results are mixed. Some studies [6, 7] have reported no evidence of a positive relation between financial performance and a proactive green strategy, while others [10] have discovered that a real commitment to green strategy can positively affect an enterprise's financial performance. Green strategy can affect the financial performance of enterprises differently, depending on whether the purpose of implementing green strategy is to improve revenue or reduce costs. The development and implementation of a proactive green strategy, for example, could lead to growth of enterprise resources including higher employee skills and enhanced reputation as an eco-friendly enterprise. Moreover, pursuing green strategy may result in some cost savings such as reducing waste materials both in production and packaging. Both approaches could ultimately increase an enterprise's profitability.

Studies focused on smaller enterprises [3] generally found those that are more proactive in pursuing a green strategy tend to be more successful. This appears to be true despite the few economic incentives that exist to help smaller enterprises to become more environmentally friendly. In addition, their limited financial resources make it more difficult for them to choose the best alternative investment that not only increase their contributions to solving ecological issues but also rewards their stockholders. Pursuing a green strategy that does not enhance the return to stockholders would have serious consequences for any enterprise especially smaller manufacturing enterprises. Therefore, the initial investments needed and the speed in recovering investments from pursuing green strategy is quite critical.

5.4   Financial Methods to Analyze Green Projects

Is there any way to distinguish between good investment projects and bad ones? Once a project has been identified, management begins the process of determining whether or not it should be pursued. Enterprises have a number of financial methods to evaluate the merit of potential projects. The more common methods used in project evaluation include net present value (NPV), internal rate of return (IRR), payback period, cost benefit analysis, break-even point, and project profitability index (PPI). The sole objective of these methods is to determine if the project would add any value to the enterprise or not. This process is called capital budgeting. It evaluates projects ranging from purchasing a piece of machinery needed for modifying a product to developing a brand new product. These methods can facilitate an enterprise's later financing decisions. These methods are described in the following section. The NPV has theoretical superiority and is described in more detail than others.

5.4.1   *Net present value method*

The NPV of a project is the sum of present values of all cash inflows from the project minus its initial investments. The NPV method applies discounted cash flow analysis that makes it very effective tool for capital budgeting analysis. The term "present value" refers to the fact that cash flows earned in the future are not worth as much as today's cash flows. Discounting those future cash flows back to the present time creates an apple-to-apple comparison between the cash flows from different projects. If an enterprise does not use the time value of money to discount cash inflows, long-term projects or those invested during high discount rate periods could be mispriced. This will lead to projects that do not add any value to the enterprise.

An enterprise evaluating long-term investments using the NPV method follows these steps:

Step 1: Estimate the expected future cash flows generated from the project.

Step 2: Assess the risk and determine a required rate of return (cost of capital) for the project. This will be used to discount the expected future cash flows.

Step 3: Compute the present value of the expected cash flows.

Step 4: Compare the present value of the expected cash flows with the initial investments. If the cash flows generated by the project exceed the required initial investments, then the project will add value to the enterprise.

5.4.1.1   *Estimate the expected future cash flows*

This step involves estimating expected incremental after-tax cash flows. Managers must be aware of three critical concepts: (1) as with any investment, the cost and benefits associated with a project must be measured in terms of cash flow rather than earnings because earnings also reflect certain noncash items; only cash flows can be distributed to stockholders; (2) cash, not earnings are required to meet the enterprise's financial obligations; (3) timing of a cash flow affects its value because of the time value of money.

Insight Box:

Your enterprise just paid $1,000,000 in cash for a warehouse as part of a new project. The entire $1,000,000 is an immediate cash outflow. Assuming your enterprise uses a straight-line depreciation method and the project is depreciated over a 20-year period, only $50,000 is considered as an accounting expense in the current year. What should you consider as your cash outflow in the current year?

Although, it is true that the current year earnings are reduced by only $50,000, and the remaining $950,000 is depreciated over the next 19 years, for capital budgeting purposes, the relevant cash outflow at time 0 (current year) is the full $1,000,000, not the reduction in earnings of $50,000.

Next is the principle of incremental benefits. In other words, the cash flows must be measured on an incremental basis. These are the difference between the enterprise's cash flows with or without the project. Any cost incurred before the accept/reject decision is made and cannot be recovered is called a "sunk cost". This means market analysis expenses and R&D expenses incurred before the investment decisions are made are both likely to be sunk costs.

Insight Box:

Your enterprise is evaluating the NPV of establishing a new line of products. As part of the evaluation, you had hired a consulting enterprise to conduct a market research analysis. The consulting company charged you $1,000,000. The expenditure incurred last year. Is this cost relevant to the decision you are considering now?

The answer is no. The $1,000,000 is not recoverable, as it has already incurred last year. So the $1,000,000 consulting cost is a sunk cost. Of course, the decision to spend $1,000,000 for a market analysis was a capital budgeting decision by itself and perfectly relevant before it was sunk. In other words, the cost became irrelevant for any future decision once you incurred the expense.

Finally, the principle of incremental benefits further requires that expected future cash flows be measured on an after-tax basis. Investors are interested in the net gain in their wealth, and taxes diminish any increase in their wealth. Remember that we assume all cash inflows happened at the end of each period unless it is explicitly stated otherwise.

5.4.1.2   *Assess the risk and determine a required rate of return*

The enterprise must evaluate the underlying sources of risk to the project by identifying factors that impact the investment and the uncertainty that describes them. After identifying these risks, the enterprise should lessen some risks while recognizing its exposure to other risks. Risks should be monitored carefully throughout the life of the project. There are techniques that the enterprise can use to assess the impact of uncertainty on project outcomes such as scenario analysis, breakeven sensitivity analysis, and Monte Carlo simulation. Unfortunately, the underlying basis for using these techniques is inherently subjective as they rely on the judgment of the person performing the analysis.

The enterprise should then determine a required rate of return for discounting expected future cash flows. We must have a discount rate to evaluate an investment project, or a cost of capital that reflects the cash flows risks. Financial experts often use terms such as opportunity cost of capital (or simply cost of capital) to describe the appropriate discount rate used to calculate the value of an investment's future cash flows. Generally, enterprises use their overall weighted average cost of capital (WACC) as the discount rate. WACC for an enterprise is its weighted average of the expected after-tax rates of return from various sources of capital. It can also be viewed as the expected rate of return that investors in the enterprise forgo from alternative investment opportunities with equal risk. This is mostly used to value an entire enterprise. Enterprises regularly track their WACC and use it as a benchmark for determining the appropriate discount rate for new investment projects or evaluating their own performance.

Insight Box:

Your enterprise owns an empty warehouse in Madison, Wisconsin that can be used to store a new line of products you plan to produce. You hope to sell these products to Midwest customers. Should you consider the warehouse as a cost in your decision to sell the products?

Yes, because if you decide not to produce the products you can sell the warehouse. This will make the price of the warehouse an opportunity cost in your investment decision.

The mechanics of calculating an enterprise's WACC can be summarized with the following procedures:

(1) Evaluate the enterprise's capital structure and determine the relative weight of each component in the mix (i.e., capital structure weights for equity, debt, and preferred stocks).
(2) Estimate the cost of each source of capital and adjust it for the effects of taxes (the interest costs on the debt instruments are tax deductible).
(3) Calculate the WACC by computing a weighted average of the estimated after-tax costs of capital sources used by the enterprise. Assuming the capital structure is financed by combination of equity, debt, and preferred stocks, the WACC can be calculated using Equation (5.1).

$$\text{WACC} = W_e r_e + W_d r_d (1 - t) + W_p r_p, \qquad (5.1)$$

where W's are the proportion of equity, debt, and preferred stocks in the capital structure, and r's are the cost of equity, after-tax cost of debt, and the dividend on preferred stocks.

The cost of equity is what investors expect in return for their investments in the enterprise. Expected returns on equity can vary significantly. For example, the industry in which an enterprise operates is an important determinant. The risk level among different industries varies, so is the expected rate of return by investors. There are two approaches to estimating the cost of equity: (1) the risk and return model (or Capital Asset Pricing Model, CAPM) and (2) the dividend-growth model.

As stated earlier, the expected return for a project is positively related to its risk. The higher the risk, the higher expected return investors expect — that is, investors will invest in a risky project only if its expected return pays off for its risk. The CAPM is built on this premise. It gives a cost of equity that is based on the beta (a measure of its systematic or none diversifiable risk) of the equity in the enterprise. The cost of equity using the Capital Asset Pricing Model is calculated using the Equation (5.2)

$$r_j = \beta(r_m - r_g), \tag{5.2}$$

where r_j = rate of return on specific security, β = beta on the same security, r_m = average rate of return on the market portfolio (generally, the rate of return on S&P500 is used as a proxy), and r_g = rate of return on government securities (risk-free securities).

In the dividend-growth model, investors consider the enterprise as a source of growing wealth. This model assumes that cash dividend payments will grow at some average growth rate per year forever. This extreme assumption may seem flawed at first since enterprises don't really last forever. However, most of a stock's price is determined by the value of its nearest dividend payments because the time value of money reduces the present value of distant cash flows substantially. Using the dividend growth model (Equation (5.3)), the cost of equity is

$$r_j = \frac{D_1}{P_0} + g, \tag{5.3}$$

where D_1 = next year dividend, P_0 = current stock price, and g is the annual rate of dividend growth.

Insight Box:

Your enterprise is considering a project that requires an initial investment of $1,000,000 that is entirely financed by equity. The

---

(Continued)

(Continued)

project has a beta 1.0 and promises a unique perpetual annual cash flow of $140,000. Currently, the return on a market portfolio (S&P 500) is 10%, and the rate of return on long-term government bonds (risk-free rate) is 5%. What is the equity required rate of return for this project using CAPM and Dividend Growth models?

Using the CAPM (Equation (5.4)), the cost of equity is

$$r_j = \beta(r_m - r_g), \tag{5.4}$$

$$r_j = 7\% + 1.0(10\% - 5\%) = 12.0\%.$$

Using the dividend growth model (Equation (5.4)), the cost of equity is

$$r_j = \frac{\$3.00}{\$37.5} + 0.04 = 12\%.$$

The interest rate that an enterprise must pay if it needs to borrow today is called the cost of debt. This rate not only represents the market interest rate but also reflects the enterprise's default risk. Since the financial conditions in the enterprise can change overtime, its cost of debt can also change, thus the interest rate used to pay on its last borrowings are no longer useful in determining its current WACC.

If the enterprise has some long-term bonds outstanding and they are traded in the market, the yield-to-maturity on those bonds can be used as a proxy for its cost of debt. For example, if the enterprise has issued a bond that is rated by credit rating agencies such as Standard and Poor's, the enterprise can use the rating and a typical default spread on bonds with that rating to estimate its cost of debt. However, if the bond is not rated by any credit rating agency but the enterprise has very recently obtained a long-term loan from a bank it can use the interest rate on that borrowing as its cost of debt. In addition, the cost of debt must be estimated in the same currency as the cost of equity, and the cash inflows generated by the project.

5.4.1.3   *Calculate the present value of future cash flows*

The third step in project evaluation focuses on calculating the present value of cash flows for the project. For project with a finite or short life, the enterprise needs to compute cash flows for the planning period followed by computing a salvage value that is the expected from selling all of the investment in the project at the end of the project's life. For project with an infinite or long life, the enterprise should compute cash flows for the planning period and then compute the present value of all cash flows that occur after the planning period ends (or terminal value). We can use Equation (5.5) to calculate the present value of future cash flows

$$PV = \frac{CF_1}{(1+r)^1} + \frac{CF_2}{(1+r)^2} + \cdots + \frac{CF_n}{(1+r)^n}, \qquad (5.5)$$

where CF_1 to CF_n are the cash inflows generated by the project, and r is the discount rate (or WACC). In the above formula CF_n also include any salvage or terminal value the enterprise recovers after the terminal year.

5.4.1.4   *Compare the present value of the expected cash flows*

In the final step, we compare the present value of the expected cash inflows with the initial cost of the project. The general rules for NPV method are very simple. Independent projects are accepted when their NPV is positive and rejected when their NPV is negative. For mutually exclusive projects, the investment with the highest NPV is accepted. Consequently, projects with positive NPV will increase the value of the enterprise, while projects with negative NPV will reduce the value of the enterprise. Equation (5.6) can be used to set up the NPV

$$NPV = \frac{CF_1}{(1+r)^1} + \frac{CF_2}{(1+r)^2} + \frac{CF_3}{(1+r)^3} - CF_0. \qquad (5.6)$$

The basic investment rule can be generalized as

Accept a project if the NPV is greater than zero,

Reject a project if the NPV is less than zero.

Insight Box:

Your enterprise is considering a project costing $15,000,000. The project is expected to generate the following cash flows: $5,000,000 in year 1, $7,500,000 in year 2, and $10,000,000 in years 3. After year 3, the project produces no more cash flows and will be abandoned. Assume the discount rate is 10 percent. What is the NPV for this project?

The present value of cash inflows from this project is equal to $3,256,949.

$$\text{NPV} = \frac{\$5,000,000}{(1+0.10)} + \frac{\$7,500,000}{(1+0.10)^2} + \frac{\$10,000,000}{(1+0.10)^3}$$
$$-\$15,000,000 = \$3,256,950.$$

Since NPV > 0, the project is acceptable.

Now assume the $15 million cash you were going to use was already invested in short-term government securities yielding 2%. Your accountant argues that the project should be charged for lost interest, amounting to $300,000 per year ($15,000,000 \times 0.02$). Is he right?

There are some issues that arise with respect to both weight and opportunity cost that need to be addressed: (1) an enterprise must always use market weights instead of book value weights of its capital structure because market values, unlike book values, represent the relative values placed on the enterprise's securities at the time of the analysis. The market value of equity should include the market value of outstanding common stocks, outstanding warrants, and conversion option in convertible bonds. (2) The enterprise must use forward-looking weights and opportunity costs. It is reasonable to assume that the weights for components of WACC are constant as long as the enterprise's financial strategies remain unchanged. However, there are circumstances where financial strategies will change in predictable ways over the life of an investment. Therefore, the weight for each component of the capital structure may change.

Insight Box:

You work for a large, diversified enterprise. In 2016, your enterprise generated 35% of its profits from the entertainment division, 30% from the computer division, and 35% came from the healthcare services division. You are evaluating a proposed project in healthcare services. You estimate your enterprise's WACC is 11%. Is this the appropriate discount rate to use for the proposed project?

For an enterprise with multiple divisions or subsidiaries the WACC represent the discount rate for the whole organization. In this case, the 11% is really an average cost of capital for the entire enterprise. Therefore, each division must use its own cost of capital reflecting the risk that is specific to that division. In case the cost of capital for each individual division is not available, we recommend that you use an estimate of the cost of capital for the new project by applying the WACC in other enterprises that operate solely in healthcare services.

5.4.2   *Internal rate of return method*

This method is used to determine how much of a return an enterprise can expect to realize from a particular investment project. It is essentially the discount rate that equates the NPV of the project to zero. In other words, it is the rate of return an enterprise earns based upon the incremental time-weighted cash inflows from the project. However, in this case, instead of applying a discount rate to the project, we calculate the rate that is required to make the NPV zero. In fact, IRR always reaches the same decision as NPV in normal cases where the initial outflows of an independent investment project are followed only by a series of inflows.

The general rules for the IRR are simple. The enterprise should choose the project where its IRR is higher than its cost of capital. For example, if the enterprise cost of capital is 5%, it does not accept projects unless the IRR is greater than 5%. Projects with the highest difference between their IRR and cost of capital are the most attractive ones.

Using this method, an enterprise can compare the rates of return expected from a range of projects against the rate of return achievable from other investments, such as depositing the money in the bank, and choose the one it would like to undertake. The IRR for a project can be set up using Equation (5.7).

$$\frac{CF_1}{(1+IRR)^1} + \frac{CF_2}{(1+IRR)^2} + \frac{CF_3}{(1+IRR)^3} - CF_0 = 0. \qquad (5.7)$$

Unfortunately, using the IRR method to evaluate mutually exclusive projects can become very tricky. Two mutually exclusive projects can produce contradictory IRRs and NPVs when the projects' initial investments are different. For example, one project can have a lower IRR but higher NPV than another project. In spite of this issue, IRR is still a very valuable method in investment decision-making process and many enterprises tend to use it. Enterprises often incline to value percentages more than numbers (i.e., an IRR of 30% versus an NPV of $1,000,000 seems easier to understand) as percentages are more meaningful in measuring project profitability.

Insight Box:

Your enterprise is again considering a project costing $15,000,000. The project is expected to generate the following cash flows: $5,000,000 in year 1, $7,500,000 in year 2, and $10,00,000 in year 3. After year 3, the project produces no more cash flows. What is the IRR for this project?

You can calculate the IRR either by trial and error that is very time consuming, or by a financial calculator.

$$\frac{\$5,000,000}{(1+IRR)^1} + \frac{\$7,500,000}{(1+IRR)^2} + \frac{\$10,000,000}{(1+IRR)^3} - \$15,000,000 = 0.$$

The IRR for this particular project is about 21%. That is at 21% the NPV of the above project is zero. Thus, if the cost of financing this project is below 21%, the project creates value under the IRR calculation; if the cost of financing is greater than 21%, the project will destroy value.

5.4.3 *Payback period method*

The payback period is a very simple decision tool for assessing the
value of a project and comparing it with similar projects. It is
the length of time that it takes for a project to recover its initial
investments. For example, if your enterprise is considering purchasing
a warehouse that is selling for $1,000,000 and it produces cash flows
of $200,000 a year, the payback period is 5 years.

The payback period is a highly effective and efficient way to
evaluate a project for enterprises that generate healthy levels of cash
flow that allow a project to recoup its investment in a few short
years. When mutually exclusive projects are evaluated, the project
with the shorter payback period should be selected. However, this
method only shows the time it takes for a project to pay for itself
but does not consider the cash flows generated from the projects
after the payback period. It also does not consider the time value of
money.

Insight Box:

Your enterprise is considering acquisition of a warehouse. There
are two warehouses available both at the cost of $500,000 and are
the same in every other respect. While Warehouse A generates
$1,000,000 in its second year of operation, Warehouse B generates
$500,000 in its first year and $250,000 in the second year of
operation. Which warehouse should your enterprise select using
the payback period method?

For mutually exclusive projects, according to the payback
period method, the enterprise should select the project with
the shortest payback period. In this case, the enterprise should
choose Warehouse B. Although both warehouses cost the same,
Warehouse B has a payback period of only one year, whereas
Warehouse A will payback in roughly one and a half years.

The above example clearly shows the limitations of the payback
period. Here the enterprise should pick Warehouse B because it had

the shorter payback period. According to NPV or IRR criterion, as shown below, the decision favors Warehouse A as it has the higher NPV and IRR values. Indeed, the NPV of Warehouse A is more than twice that of Warehouse B that implies that Warehouse A is a greatly superior project.

$$\text{NPV}_{\text{Warehouse A}} = \frac{\$1000,000}{(1+0.10)^2} - \$500,000 = \$326,446$$

$$\text{IRR}_{\text{Warehouse A}} = 41\%,$$

$$\text{NPV}_{\text{Warehouse B}} = \frac{\$500,000}{(1+0.10)^1} + \frac{\$250,000}{(1+0.10)^2} - \$500,000 = \$16,1156$$

$$\text{IRR}_{\text{Warehouse B}} = 37\%.$$

5.4.4 *Cost benefit analysis*

This method is most suitable for evaluating of large infrastructure and public projects. It can also be used by businesses working within a consortium to deliver a major project. This method employs a discounted cash flow method in order to evaluate the social and economic benefits generated by a project. This method requires the enterprise to measure the impact of the project on the organization. For example, they need to evaluate whether the new project could be staffed by assigning overtime to current employe or should the enterprise hire additional staff? Does it make more sense to invest funds in a new project rather than investing them in government securities? It is more appropriate for evaluating projects that require small capital investments and short term in nature.

5.4.5 *Break-even point method*

The break-even point method is frequently used to evaluate an investment project where the cumulative net cash flow is equal to zero. At that point, all cash inflows have covered cash outflows. The advantage of this method is that the shorter the time to break-even the less risk that may gravely affect the estimates employed in cash flow projections. The downside of this method is that it entirely ignores the probability of more returns after the break-even point and therefore is not a good gauge of a project's real potential.

5.4.6   *Project profitability index*

Smaller enterprises with limited sources of funds may also use the PPI to decide which project they prefer. It requires the enterprise to divide NPV of the project by the amount of initial investment. The results indicate the NPV generated from every dollar of investment. The general rule is very simple: choose projects with the higher PPI, as they are more attractive.

Typically, most US enterprises use either NPV or IRR methods. This is not surprising given the theoretical advantages of these approaches. There are other methods that may be used, such as Payback period and cost benefit analysis, break-even point, total cost, or PPI, *albeit* by fewer enterprises. While these alternative methods have some redeeming qualities, when all is said and done, they are not the NPV rule or IRR, and their conceptual problems make them decidedly second rate.

5.5   Practical Issues with the Use of Investment Decision Rules

The conclusions on a project are clearly conditioned by a large number of assumptions about cash inflows, costs, and other variables over a very long period of time — all of which could be inaccurate. An enterprise may gain more confidence in these conclusions by checking how sensitive the decision measures (NPV, IRR, etc.) are to changes in key assumptions used in the analysis. We always assume enterprises use NPV, IRR, or payback period decision rules; in reality, many enterprises do not follow those rules. For example, in the case of acquiring a warehouse, as presented earlier, assume NPV of Warehouse A was only slightly higher than that of Warehouse B, yet the enterprise might be concerned about meeting its upcoming financial obligations. As a result, the enterprise may decide to acquire Warehouse B because it provides quicker upfront cash flows but has a lower return. Why would an enterprise make such a decision?

It is quite possible that the enterprise has to borrow a large portion of its initial investment and would like to pay back the loan soon in order to save on interest expense. This would make the project with a quicker payback period more attractive than the one with slightly higher NPV.

Many enterprise managers tend to place greater emphasis on the accounting implications of their investment decision rather than on the projects' NPVs. It is not unusual to pass up projects with a positive NPV that would briefly decrease their enterprises' earnings and lower their own annual compensation packages as a result. These problems generally arise when managerial performance is regularly evaluated by changes in an enterprise's earnings. This encourages managers to select new investment projects based on whether they are accretive or dilutive to the enterprise's earnings. This leads to a number of issues:

1. *Cost of equity issue.* This issue is related to the appropriate cost of equity in project evaluations. It reveals that earnings per share (EPS) do not consider the appropriate cost of equity. What if the project is riskier? Should we still use the cost of equity to evaluate a project? This problem can be eliminated if the enterprise depends more on its economic profit than earnings.

2. *Back-loaded versus front-loaded earnings.* This issue reflects the fact that some projects may receive most of their cash flows later in life (back-loaded earnings). This may result in the enterprise having lower EPS in early years of the project but still have positive NPVs. Similarly, projects with front-loaded cash flows may cause an enterprise to have higher EPS in the early years of project life but negative NPVs. Unfortunately, by choosing projects with front-loaded cash flows, thereby maximizing their short-term profitability enterprises put both shareholder value and stakeholder interests at risk, hence unable to maximize their shareholders' wealth. In such cases, enterprises need to revise their economic profit to reflect economic depreciation and also capitalize research and development costs, and advertising expenses by amortizing them over the project life. In addition,

compensating their managers appropriately and communicating the long-term value of their investments to the capital markets should alleviate these concerns. The problem is in persuading financial markets that the numbers reported really reflect an enterprise's true performance. The financial markets generally do not believe the current earnings are low because the enterprise is making investments that will pay off in the future.

As a general rule, managers must keep in mind that all investment decisions should be made based on creating value for the shareholders. In the example above, Warehouse A must be selected because it generates significantly higher value for the enterprise's shareholders. Consequently, accepting any project with lower NPV results in destroying shareholder value.

5.6   How to Finance Green Projects

Any capital budgeting choice involves two sets of decisions: investment decisions and financial decisions. An enterprise makes a project investment decisions not only based on profitability and feasibility but also based on its ability to raise needed capital to finance the project. An investment project that generates positive NPV is considered financially viable because it adds to the enterprise valuation and eventually to stockholders' wealth. The important question is how enterprises finance their investment projects.

Enterprises have a number of tools in their disposal in order to forecast their funding needs for investment projects. But what is the best source of funds? In addition to internal sources of funds, some enterprises may have access to external sources, such as debt or equity. This raises the issue of whether the enterprise has an ideal capital structure, i.e., an optimal mix between debt and equity. Can an enterprise add value to its stockholders' wealth by following a good financing mix? If yes, does the optimal financial mix depend on the enterprise's operations (real investment policy) and how?

In general, enterprises that believe their stocks are overvalued or they do not generate high enough profits to worry about taxes and also have highly erratic cash flows tend to prefer using equity as their source of financing. On the other hand, enterprises that believe their equity is highly undervalued in the current financial market conditions or care more about their taxes and can generate very stable cash flows tend to use debt. These enterprises may not have any specific target debt ratio. Should any enterprise consider 100% debt financing? Although the tax benefits of using debt dominate at a low leverage ratio, costs related to financial distress increase dramatically at a high leverage. The additional cost of financial distress exceeds the tax benefits from carrying an additional debt ratio at a certain point.

There are numerous direct and indirect costs related to financial distress. They include: management's time and effort alongside the legal costs of dealing with bankruptcy issues, indirect costs such as foregone positive NPV projects, loss of competitive position, loss of customers, loss of suppliers, asset fire sales and liquidation, and loss of interest tax shields. These trade-offs lead to an optimal capital structure. Generally, enterprises that face a high probability of financial distress should not consider a heavy debt load. They have a tendency to own more fixed assets that cannot be sold easily or own a high level of intangible assets. Enterprises with high growth potential and time-sensitive investments should not consider high leverage in their capital structure. Additionally, enterprises with risky earnings and cash flows — which lead to high probability of financial distress — and those with low earnings and cumulative losses — which reduce any tax advantage for the enterprise — should not consider high leverage in their capital structure.

Insight Box:

Your enterprise needs to raise capital in order to finance a new project. Should your enterprise use retained earnings, issue debt, or equity?

In general, enterprises prefer internal to external financing. In case of external financing, enterprises prefer debt to equity. The tax deductibility of interest costs lowers cost of debt and gives it

---

(*Continued*)

(Continued)

an advantage over equity. However, this preference is not universal across industries. Industries that usually generate more stable cash flows are capable of having higher debt loads than industries whose cash flows are less predictable. That is why high tech enterprises have very little debt in their capital structure compared to public utilities.

Another critical issue with respect to financing a project is the impact of financing decisions on the value of current shareholders wealth. While stock prices react negatively to new equity issues as it dilutes an enterprise's EPS, they react positively to bank loans and very little to public debt issues. For example, issuing new stocks to finance a new project would lead to the dilution of an enterprise's EPS and lead to a lower price for outstanding stocks and loss of corporate control due to more shares outstanding. In addition, underwriting costs of issuing new stocks far exceed the costs of issuing new debt instruments.

Ultimately, a correct financing decision must ensure that funds are available, both today and in the future, for positive NPV investment projects. While equity provides more flexibility, debt is more restrictive and, in extreme cases, can lead to bankruptcy. Moreover, smaller manufacturing enterprises' access to outside capital is very limited, and often a simple product modification can become a difficult endeavor.

Recommended Readings

1. Berry, M. A. and Rondinelli, D. A. (1998). "Proactive Corporate Environmental Management: A New Industrial Revolution." *The Academy of Management Executive* 12, 38–50.
2. Bianchi, R. and Noci, G. (1998). "'Greening' SMEs Competitiveness." *Small Business Economics* 11, 269–281.
3. Clemens, B. (2006). "Economic Incentives and Small Firms: Does it Pay to be Green?" *Journal of Business Research* 59, 492–500.
4. Cramer, J. (1998). "Environmental Management: From 'Fit' to 'Stretch.'" *Business Strategy and the Environment* 7, 162–172.

5. Dewhurst, P. (1993). "Product Design for Manufacture: Design for Disassembly." *Industrial Engineering* 25, 26–28.

6. Gilley, K., Worrell, D., Davidson III, W. and El-Jelly, A. (2000). "Corporate Environmental Initiatives and Anticipated Firm Performance: The Differential Effects of Process-Driven Versus Product-Driven Greening Initiatives." *Journal of Management* 26, 1199–216.

7. Link, S. and Naveh, E. (2006). "Standardization and Discretion: Does the Environmental Standard ISO 14001 Lead to Performance Benefits?" *IEEE Transactions on Engineering Management* 53, 508–519.

8. Maxwell, J., Rothenberg, S., Briscoe, F. and Marcus, A. (2002). "Green Schemes: Corporate Environmental Strategies and Their Implementation." *California Management Review* 39, 118–134.

9. Moini, H., Sørensen, O. J. and Szuchy Kristiansen, E. (2014). "Adoption on Green Strategy by Danish Firms." *Sustainability Accounting and Management Policy Journal* 5, 197–223.

10. Zhu, Q. and Sarkis, J. (2004). "Relationships Between Operational Practices and Performance Among Early Adopters of Green Supply Chain Management Practices in Chinese Manufacturing Enterprises." *Journal of Operations Management* 22, 265–289.

Chapter 6

Competitive Positioning Subject to Green Marketing Strategies

Smaller manufacturing enterprises, to a large extent, base their competitive positioning on financial and marketing strategies. The financial strategy is the strength of financial resources and the extent to which the enterprise can fulfill its commitment to green initiatives. The marketing strategy is the process the enterprise uses to implement its commitment to green initiatives by marketing green products and services to green consumers. The financial and marketing strategies are managerial tools designed by the enterprise to compete so it realizes its mission and utilizes its resources effectively and efficiently.

Commitments to green initiatives vary significantly among smaller manufacturing enterprises from total commitment which focuses an entire enterprise on executing and implementing green activities and marketing its green products and services to green consumers to artificially pretending to offer green products and services. Enterprises totally committed to green initiates follow managerial philosophies and develop green marketing strategies that reflect their green commitment. Enterprises that commit less to green initiatives formulate green marketing strategies that emphasize different marketing activities, such as green promotional efforts or packaging among other approaches. A green marketing strategy is constrained by the financial strategy that reflects the green commitment and has a direct bearing on competitive position.

Competitive positioning by smaller manufacturing enterprises needs to be understood the range and scope of green marketing initiatives and activities. Many smaller manufacturing enterprises define their markets and corresponding activities as local while other enterprises define their markets as regional or national. More-advanced enterprises, especially high-technology enterprises, define their market as their international. The commitment to green marketing reflects how an enterprise defines its competitive position regardless of its market orientation.

For example, a local fabrication shop of solar electric and water heating panels for private residences, in a narrowly defined geographic region, is fully committed to green initiatives. Solar panels of their own design power their fabricating facilities. Their engineers and technicians serve the local solar technology in their community; all marketing and sales activities emphasize their local orientation and dedication to solar power. This can be contrasted with an internationally oriented enterprise that manufactures of institutional cleaning products and differentiates among foreign markets depending on local cleaning practices and commitments to green products. Such an enterprise markets products based on local market demand for green products and includes only ingredients necessary to meet local requirements for such products.

In defining competitive positions, smaller manufacturing enterprises are influenced by their geographic orientation. A competitive position may be directly related to market factors and conditions such as the age of the market or the character of products or services used. For example, depending on the age of an industry, demand for green products or services may be limited. It would be difficult for an industry at the end of its life cycle to introduce green products or services and successfully integrate them into the aging industry. Conversely, it is less economically and technologically demanding for an industry at the beginning of its life cycle to introduce innovative recycled materials, design electronic components that conserve energy, use equipment that emit less noise or otherwise present a small carbon footprint.

Consumer expectations can play a major role in determining the appropriate competitive position for smaller manufacturing enterprises. Consumers know intuitively which green products or services they need to construct their green lifestyles. Consumers committed to green lifestyles are more likely to purchase electric cars and rechargeable lawn mowers or consume nondurable products packaged in recyclable packaging. The same consumers recycle as much waste as they possibly can and demand waste collection capabilities from local municipalities, and in some cases, choose to live in green communities. Other consumers, less committed to green consumption, may purchase a hybrid automobile because hybrid automobiles have inherent visibility as being green. Consumers with a passing interest in green issues may purchase conventional automobiles based on fuel consumption ratings, and only if driving conditions necessitate such a decision because of personal economies.

Consumers' expectations and consumption behaviors offer green marketing flexibility for smaller manufacturing enterprises. Depending on its level of commitment to green initiatives, an enterprise may identify a market segment closely aligned with its level of green marketing commitment. The alignment between consumers and enterprises is a major factor in how an enterprise defines its competitive position. Managers of some smaller manufacturing enterprises, especially local low technology enterprises, suggest that their consumers provide the necessary input into how their green commitment needs to change and how their competitive position needs to adjust.

6.1 Specification of a Competitive Position

Specifying a competitive position by a smaller manufacturing enterprise marketing products and services in competitive markets requires assessment of its marketing advantage and financial potential. The concept of a competitive platform is a suitable tool used in specifying the competitive position of an enterprise. A competitive platform consists of a series of sequential decisions made by marketing managers and reviewed by financial managers since the competitive positioning decision is dependent on innovative approaches developed by marketing managers and financial limitations set by financial managers. An enterprise must define its marketing advantage and its financial strength in order to build a solid competitive platform. Such a definition is essential to selecting its competitors and determining its competitive position.

No single set of procedures, models, or tools can be used to define competitive position for individual smaller manufacturing enterprises. There is a heuristic approach to how decision makers set competitive positions. One approach is to build a competitive platform on which decisions can be made to compete in dynamic markets. Managers agree that common components may be used in building a competitive platform from which a competitive position can be defined. They agree that each competitive platform is unique and reflects the managerial philosophy of each enterprise.

The following are some of the components that make up a competitive platform. The first component is a process designed to identify competitors — more specifically, with whom is the enterprise able to compete? This decision is based on an assumption in marketing management that an enterprise identifies and selects its competitors. The second component determines the level on which an enterprise is willing and able to compete — its innovative ability, products or services, production efficiency or capability, level of managerial commitments, or long-term strategic focus, among other options. Availability of resources determines the ability to compete on a given level. The third component is to define products and services that become the competitive factors in a marketing strategy. The fourth component is the focus on consumers or users. The fifth component is the qualitative and quantitative approaches employed to identify and select market segments. The final component is the specification of markets in which the enterprise will compete.

Once an enterprise has the necessary information to decide its optimal competitive position, implementation of a competitive position is generally accomplished through a systematically formulated marketing strategy. A marketing management perspective among smaller manufacturing enterprises suggests that competition is a constraint on marketing strategy and can be strategically managed with marketing philosophies, innovative marketing approaches, and astute management of enterprise resources. Many managers of high-technology enterprises perceive their competitive positions as additional means of specifying their market strengths. Conversely, their market strengths help them maintain solid competitive positions.

6.1.1 *Geographic competitive relationships*

Smaller manufacturing enterprises construct their competitive positioning strategies on several levels. In geographic competitive positioning, managers perceive their competitive space as geographically defined. Smaller manufacturing enterprises are locally, regionally, or nationally oriented. Geographic orientation is often connected with the type of products or services marketed by an enterprise and is limited by managerial philosophies and strategic goals and objectives. Many top managers, especially those managing privately owned enterprises, base the geographic boundaries for their marketing initiatives on personal preferences. As enterprises grow and expand their markets, mainly due to growing demand for their products or a need to reach outside their traditional markets, they expand their geographic preferences.

Geographically oriented enterprises that reach outside their traditional markets, require additional competitive knowledge. Some enterprises receive competitive information from consumers who create new demand for products or services from other geographically delineated markets. Internet marketing, for example, enables consumers to cross geographic boundaries and confront smaller manufacturing enterprises to expand, locally, regionally, or internationally. The other extreme of geographic orientation is when a foreign consumer approaches a smaller regional manufacturing enterprise and asks to purchase a product displayed on the webpage of the regionally oriented enterprise.

Competitive relationships among smaller manufacturing enterprises are dynamic and need to be defined by the broadest perspective possible since a webpage posted on the Internet, is not geographically limited. Consumers do not recognize geographic orientation among smaller manufacturing enterprises even though some managers limit their focus to local markets and are reluctant to sell products or services outside their subjectively defined markets. It is the value and utility of a product or service to the ultimate consumer that determine demand.

Some smaller high-technology manufacturing enterprises operate internationally, often from their founding. An enterprise located in a geographically remote region of the world may have customers dispersed throughout the world. For example, specialized garden tools manufactured in a rural area have a reputation of quality among gardeners worldwide. The manufacturer ships orders daily to remote parts of the world. Some smaller manufacturing enterprises are internationally focused startups depending on the level of technology, managerial philosophy, or top managers' objectives.

Managers of smaller manufacturing enterprises suggest that the notion of competitive space is mostly related to top decision makers' managerial philosophy. Nevertheless, some managers differentiate geographically in their market philosophies as local, regional, national, and international, while other managers classify markets as being domestic or foreign. Very few managers initially see markets as international.

Managers among smaller manufacturing enterprises do not form competitive positions on geographic perspectives. Competitive relationships among smaller manufacturing enterprises serve as partial frameworks within which competitive positions are specified. From a marketing management perspective, specification of a competitive position reaches beyond the types of markets defined by top decision makers. Managers believe that controllable marketing variables define competitive positions. Although each enterprise perceives the importance of individual controllable variables differently, managers recognize similar marketing variables. Managers also suggest the controllable marketing variables in marketing strategies may limit the specification of individual competitive positions.

6.1.2   *Marketing competitive relationships*

Top decision makers may consider a number of strategic marketing variables as input when formulating a competitive position. These generally include strategic variables for the entire enterprise regardless of the products or services the enterprise markets. This approach is particularly important for enterprises with broad missions and strategic flexibility. For example, as a high-technology enterprise grows and responds to market needs, it has options as to which additional markets to enter and on what technological level. A smaller manufacturing enterprise of specialized industrial computers has a wide range of options as to which supply chains to enter or even what industry to serve because the component it supplies is only an incidental part of the finished product. Industrial computers are components of many consumer products and an enterprise may formulate several substantially different competitive positions depending on the end markets.

There are differing approaches for formulating competitive positions among smaller manufacturing enterprises given the perspective of marketing managers today — marketing is the main operating philosophy. Some approaches are subjective and represent different perspectives of marketing, they are viewed by top decision makers as effective in formulating strong competitive positions.

Perhaps the most important variable on which a strong strategic competitive position can be formulated is the capability of an enterprise to consistently and systematically innovate. The ability to innovate needs to flow throughout an enterprise. Its innovative capabilities must be embedded in its mission and built into every product or service it markets. Marketing activities must be innovative and reflect the overall innovative philosophy and force of the enterprise. The specific definition of how an enterprise innovates must be clearly contained within its competitive position — it innovates through the ideas of experts it employs and innovative products based on sound scientific inventions built into technologically efficient and effective products.

Managers of smaller manufacturing enterprises suggest that competitive positions can be formulated based on their marketing expertise. Marketing expertise is a reformulation of the mission and management philosophy of the enterprise, represents an understanding of consumers, markets, and competitors, and uses this understanding to design a unique competitive position. However, some marketing managers among smaller manufacturing enterprises point out that marketing expertise is an abstract notion and difficult to define.

Competitive positions can be formulated based on how competitors perceive each other. Market followers frequently copy smaller manufacturing enterprises that behave as market innovators. Market innovators typically introduce new concepts or ideas in various markets. The products or services they develop may not be major innovations; however, the introduction to a market or markets is innovative because the promotion or distribution is new or a product or service is used or performs in a different way. Market followers quickly imitate market innovators; thus, market innovators must define their competitive positions effectively to maintain their competitive positions over time.

Some smaller manufacturing enterprises approach formulating a competitive position passively because they do not have the financial strength to compete. They watch competitors compete over markets and, when appropriate, assess the competitors' strengths and weaknesses and then reexamine their own competitive positions. Managers of high-technology, smaller manufacturing enterprises think that technological innovations offer better potential for creating a strong competitive position than financial strength. Enterprises with financial strengths often market products or services based on older technology and innovate by acquiring competitive options through mergers or acquisitions; high-technology enterprises usually innovate internally in order to gain a better competitive position.

Competitively passive smaller manufacturing enterprises without either strong financial or technological advantages are faced with three fundamental alternatives. They can seek new markets for their products or services. This approach suggests entry into new geographical markets, including foreign markets or, entry into markets with new applications for their products or services; however, its competitive position may be temporary. The second alternative for a competitively passive enterprise is to upgrade its products and services by changing product and service attributes and repositioning them in existing markets. An example of this approach is using a communication channel to create a new image, suggest new uses, or point out differences between or among competitors. This approach is competitively weak and usually short lived. The final alternative for an enterprise is to diversify into markets by purchasing ongoing ventures; the newly purchased ventures may or may not be related to its current operations. For example, an enterprise with a passive competitive position and minimally sufficient financial resources marketing noncompetitive products or services may acquire an enterprise with a completely different management philosophy and marketing initiatives.

Competitively passive smaller manufacturing enterprises are frequently compared to competitively aggressive enterprises. This comparison is important because it illustrates the extreme between the two approaches used by marketing managers of smaller manufacturing enterprises to determine competitive position as part of the managerial philosophy. Competitively aggressive enterprises can be considered market innovators. They enter markets quickly with products or services that satisfy immediate demand. If a new trend or fashion emerges, competitively aggressive enterprises enter the marker almost instantly with products or services from any possible source. Financially strong enterprises are more likely to source products or services globally or, in some instances purchase, an ongoing venture with the ability to supply the products or services they need. Competitively aggressive enterprises without necessary financial resources join supply chains, form joint ventures, or enter mergers.

Smaller manufacturers enterprises that maintain competitive market positions — generally referred to as competitive market position maintainers — are neither competitively passive nor aggressive enterprises. Such enterprises set their competitive positions to meet changing market conditions. They monitor competitors' market activities and respond when their own competitive market position is threatened. For example, a regional enterprise producing a line of green products for maintaining residential lawns and sold directly to consumers competes with national branded products labeled as green. The regional enterprise communicates directly with its customer base to learn how satisfied they are and answers any questions or address concerns consumers might have. If and when the national competitors introduce a new product or improve an existing product, the regional enterprise follows up with its customers to inform them that their products have the same characteristics and accomplish the same results. The fundamental strength of such an enterprise is its ability to communicate with consumers directly and almost instantaneously and thus foster consumers' loyalty.

A minority of smaller manufacturing enterprises formulates competitive market positions by "catching up". Managers maintain a competitive position and wait until competitors overtly set new competitive positions. Once an enterprise practicing the "catching up" approach understands its competitors' new positions, it sets a margin within which it follows the competitors' positions. An enterprise using this approach perceives the margin it sets as safe and consistent with its ability to compete.

6.1.3   *Market position and competitive advantage*

The overwhelming majority of smaller manufacturing enterprises are convinced that their products and services determine their competitive market positions or simply market positions. They consider the attributes of products and services as responsible for how they are competitively positioned in the market — the functional, physical, and psychological attributes of products and functional and psychological attributes of services. The market position of products and services is a meeting of the marketing strategies formulated by marketing managers and product and service acceptance by consumers. Many managers, especially those of high-technology, smaller manufacturing enterprises, point out that marketing positions are identified and owned by the enterprise. Others, especially those with a strong marketing management commitment, argue that market positions are created and owned by consumers.

Market position is constructed based on competitive advantages. Factors inherent in each enterprise as created by a top decision maker or reflected in the collective managerial philosophy of management determine the competitive advantage of smaller manufacturing enterprises. Managers of smaller manufacturing enterprises suggest that their unique managerial philosophies — their abilities to comprehend market conditions and consumers' willingness and ability to purchase their products and services create market positions. However, there are specific factors in marketing philosophies that provide the basic approaches needed to develop competitive advantage. Unique managerial philosophies among managers of smaller manufacturing enterprises provide the basic approach or framework for formulation of a competitive advantage. The factors within an individual philosophy become the essential tools for formulating a competitive advantage and can be defined as follows.

Among smaller manufacturing enterprises, the most important component of competitive advantage is their managerial skills. Managerial skills are closely followed by marketing skills which represent the ability to conceptualize, develop, test, and introduce unique products and services in consumer-driven and potentially profitable markets. Not every enterprise subscribes to this notion. High-technology enterprises, especially startups, often present solutions to a problem that are not yet perceived by markets. Markets need to be made aware of latent needs in such situations. Similar conditions exist among craftsman-type enterprises if a craftsman offers a product and waits until a market forms around it. In both cases, an owner–manager in a role of an entrepreneur prefers to focus on the product or service rather than the market. Such owner–managers often believe that their products are unique and consumers will eventually find them.

An enterprise seeking a new and differentiated marketing opportunity will commit to a market with the expectation that such commitment will result in a strong competitive position. Market commitments are exemplified by fads, fashions, and trends and need to be assessed and considered in the context of a long-term marketing strategy. A temporary phenomenon does not typically offer potential for a long-term strategy.

Managers of smaller green manufacturing enterprises agree that green initiatives and the market segments that form around them suggest a long-term growing phenomenon that requires market commitment. Market segments for green products and services offer innovative opportunities that become increasingly more interrelated and sequential and provide the foundation for formulating strong competitive market positions. For example, a small manufacturer of lighting fixtures offers green options for consumers — various efficient light sources. This is closely followed by offering the ability to control the fixtures with motion sensors, voice commands, or by a remote-control from a smart telephone, and then an integrated computer-based home management system. Each approach represents a unique market segment that may be evolving into a comprehensive sequential market for computer based home lighting management systems.

Innovation is the main driving force behind competitive advantage. Both managerial and marketing skills rely on the ability of an enterprise to innovate. Innovation, for many smaller manufacturing enterprises, means creating new product or service options for consumers. Managers who subscribe to this approach to innovation suggest that an enterprise must understand how their products or services will evolve technologically in the future and consistently strive to keep up with their development. High-technology startups founded on a scientific discovery, invention, or new application enter markets with innovation and market advantage. Other enterprises may perceive innovation as application of incremental technology to their products and services resulting in attribute improvements.

Examining the new product or service development abilities of smaller manufacturing enterprises offers another insight into formulating a competitive position. There seem to be two approaches among smaller manufacturing enterprises in their efforts to develop new products or services. The first is an unstructured approach with different functional specialists participating and offering products and services not fully developed and tested. Such enterprises expect their customers, consumers, or users to provide the feedback needed to improve the product. This approach relies on outside input that is frequently negative and destructive to the enterprise but is often practiced by smaller, locally oriented enterprises.

Another new product or service development effort among smaller manufacturing enterprises centers around a comprehensive approach based on results from marketing research studies — information often provided by engineering consulting agencies or other consultants. The process begins with formulating a new product or service idea, followed by specifying a comprehensive product or service concept. Both the idea and concept are analyzed and evaluated internally and a prototype is developed for a viable product or service. The prototype is tested, converted into a market acceptable product or service, and introduced to the market. Systematic development of new products or services assures market acceptability and a close match between the market approach and consumer acceptance that build the foundations for a strong competitive position.

Market position and competitive advantage are closely connected and result directly from an individual managerial philosophy. Three levels of competitive positioning emerge when examined from the perspectives of smaller manufacturing enterprises subscribing to marketing management practices. First, managers define the marketing opportunities in terms of potential consumers and their needs. Second, managers define potential markets based on the similar or collective behavior of potential consumers and specify individual market segments. Finally, managers proceed to develop products or services for selected market segments. This approach is best suited for development of green products and services.

6.1.4 *External analysis*

Developing green products or services with the intention of specifying competitive position depends on analyses external to a smaller manufacturing enterprise. If an enterprise plans to develop competitive green products or services, it must understand external conditions relevant to the enterprise. Enterprise managers must understand emerging green trends and formulate conceptual definitions of future events. This requires understanding how evolving new technology relates to its mission, managerial philosophy, and competitive position; constant monitoring and scanning of technological developments is essential.

Constant monitoring and scanning of technological developments produce information that may lead to managerial insight. Managers need to compare the potential opportunities managerial insight suggests and compare them to potential threats the enterprise faces. Although several models are available to managers for conducting such comparisons, managers feel this is often an intuitive and sometimes subjective process, especially in lower-technology, smaller manufacturing enterprises.

The trends and future events systematically analyzed and evaluated can still be confronted by expected or unexpected uncertainties. Many external events result from market discontinuities, legislative actions, or competitive pressures. Smaller manufacturing enterprises must constantly monitor the external events that may shape and potentially change their competitive positions.

Smaller manufacturing enterprises aware of external changes need to gather information. Depending on the nature of its technological base, an enterprise needs past, present, and future information concerning its competitive position. This is primarily to document and compare its competitive performance and project its position. Managers need such information to formulate approaches, projections, or computer-based scenarios to determine optimal future competitive positions. This approach answers two fundamental questions — where to compete and how to compete in the future given changing events around the enterprise.

6.2   Competitive Positions and Technological Capabilities

Competitive positioning is closely related to green consumers' expectations of the technological capabilities of smaller manufacturing enterprises in green markets. Green enterprises must demonstrate that they are at the cutting edge of technology and have the capability to develop products and services based on the latest green technologies due to consumer-driven demand or market pull. Consumers' expectations are only half of the equation in formulating competitive market positions. The other half is the latent, unknown, and unpredictable consumer expectations that cannot be articulated. Some consumers have problems for which solutions cannot be provided. Unpredictable expectations of consumers are researched, studied, or otherwise scientifically explored resulting in marginal results. In such situations, an enterprise may try to develop technologically challenging innovative products or services not fully understood by consumers that may solve current or future consumption needs. These situations represent technology-driven markets or market push.

6.2.1 *Consumer motivations*

Consumers are motivated by the value perceived in desirable product or service attributes and reflected in the latest technological aspects. Perceived product or service values stimulate buying behavior and lead to purchases. Consumers' motivations, especially motivations for technologically innovative products or services, lead consumers to seek information and set purchase priorities. For example, the decision to purchase an electric car is a complex long-term decision for many green consumers. They become aware of electric cars, not necessarily hybrid automobiles, search for more information, and explore how an electric car could fit their consumptions process and lifestyle. They become motivated, at some point, to purchase an electric car if they perceive positive personal and social outcomes from the decision.

Green consumers inevitably have unmet needs due to economic or other social constraints. Unmet need among green consumers is a complex notion from a technological perspective that has been studied only recently. Specific issues have been identified and consist of a number of unanswered questions. Green consumers tend to be dissatisfied with environmental trends and market conditions. They are concerned about consumption of nonrenewable resources. Green dissatisfaction leads to consumption of green products and services as sought after options that are at least partially green but preferably completely green.

Green consumers are often dissatisfied with packaging technology; they expect products to be protected and shipped in containers made of recyclable materials. They also expect manufacturers to take full responsibility for the containers after deliver delivery of the product — particularly when consumers buy via the Internet. Many green consumers expect that the technology for dealing efficiently and effectively with recycling packing materials exists, but think enterprises are reluctant to implement it due to cost consideration. Managers of smaller manufacturing enterprises judge many of these expectations as unrealistic. They expect, however, that they will face these and similar expectations in the future and consider them as consumers' unmet needs.

Unmet needs, especially technologically based unmet needs, are difficult to identify. It is difficult for marketing managers among smaller manufacturing enterprises to deal with future technological issues of which green consumers are not aware. Recent technological trends in power generation, packaging, transportation, and other industries impacted by major technological developments suggest that green consumers' future unmet needs will have an enormous impact on the competitive position of smaller manufacturing enterprises.

Top decision makers and marketing managers of smaller manufacturing enterprises need to understand the ramifications of technology and its relationship to competitive positioning. It is necessary to develop a comprehensive perspective regarding green consumers — understand the green behavior of their largest consumers, what motivates them, and why they are profitable. The largest green consumers generate market dynamics that tend to drive technological improvements. They are motivated to keep purchasing technologically improved or new green products and services frequently because they feel socially empowered to do so. They are willing to pay higher prices for technologically advanced green products and services. Examples can be seen in energy consumption, water use, energy-efficient appliances, and in home ownership and maintenance where technologically advanced applications allow owners to communicate with their homes to manage energy, enhance safety, and generate a less demanding lifestyle.

Marketing managers of smaller manufacturing enterprises need to understand green consumers' current needs and future unmet needs, group them into market segments, and address them directly to formulate a competitive market position. Many characteristics of green consumers can be identified and quantified. However, a predominance of behavioral factors cannot be quantified and need to be observed and subjectively factored into competitive market positioning decisions. Managers need to understand the motivations of green consumers to track the technological development of green products and services. These factors become major inputs in formulating green marketing strategies and play a dominant role in competitive market positioning.

Recommended Reading

1. Aaker, D. A. (2005). *Strategic Market Management*, 7th edition (John Wiley & Sons, Inc., Hoboken, NJ).

Chapter 7

Emerging Green Concerns and Managers of Smaller Manufacturing Enterprises

Awareness of green concerns among consumers is rapidly expanding worldwide. Changes in consumption of products and services range from industrial uses to personal consumption. Consumer concerns include energy conservation, use of chemicals that present a danger to nature, use of nonrenewable resources, and the carbon footprints of their own consumption, among other environmental concerns. In complex, highly dynamic, and technologically laden markets, consumers' escalating concerns over green issues include the growing demand for green products and services and their distribution. Green consumers worldwide are reexamining their consumption habits and how they can safely dispose of the remains of products and services, especially green products and services. This evolving post-consumption behavior has become a challenge for smaller manufacturing enterprises.

The concerns of green consumers also include recycling material waste that can be reused, conserving energy, reducing use of nonrenewable resources — most essentially drinking water, and limiting urban air pollution; eliminating mass burning of farmers' fields after harvest is fundamental to green consumers. Consumption and post-consumption of green products and services are built on these convictions. Green consumers look for products and services that underscore their green concerns such as efficient home appliances.

They look for products manufactured from recycled materials that can be further recycled at the end of their life cycles, and they prefer products or services that are functionally and psychologically engaging such as electric cars — for engaged green consumers, efficient home appliances are necessities. Much of packaging today is recyclable, but green consumers point out that recycling options are not always available.

Consumers' influences regarding green issues are more limited in economically, socially, or technologically challenged markets. Although consumers in such markets have concerns over green issues, they typically do not have the means or ways to influence demand for green products or services. Green concerns in such markets are often addressed from a societal perspective on systemic levels rather than on the consumer level. Typical systemic green concerns are public availability of unpolluted drinking water, generation of energy by solar cells or wind power, and eliminating the use of inefficient and polluting diesel powered public transports. Other concerns include the burning of organic and highly polluting fuels and highly polluting scooters and motorcycles using two cycle engines that create major health issues and environmental problems for growing cities in Africa and Asia.

Green products and services are often introduced by default in some consumer markets where green concerns are minimized for various economic and social reasons. Some manufacturers offer green consumer products and services uniformly in all the markets they serve. For example, a brand name manufacturer markets green nonpolluting products in reusable and recyclable containers in all markets. Some consumers may not be aware that the products are known as green products, even though they are actively sought after by informed green consumers. Regular nongreen consumers buy the products because the containers are safe and can be reused. In other instances, green consumers in these markets prefer air-dried herbs, coffee beans, or teas over mass produced, inefficiently kiln dried equivalents and actively look for them. Green consumers in such markets started to examine benefits of green products and services are motivated to purchase them.

Consumer markets worldwide seek green products and services. The Internet and modern telecommunication infrastructure offer green consumers a variety of choices for purchasing green products or services, and retail sources of green products are expanding internationally. Green consumers can source green products from nontraditional suppliers; similar situations exist in markets for green services. Energy-efficient construction services provided directly to consumers across national boundaries are readily available. Advisory services on how to become a green consumer are available via the Internet or in person, internationally. Managers of smaller manufacturing enterprises need to recognize the challenge and realize that green opportunities are ubiquitous and require innovative approaches to markets.

7.1   Market Responses by Smaller Manufacturing Enterprises

The responses of marketing managers of smaller manufacturing enterprises to green challenges are limited by the commitment of their own enterprises to green initiatives and consumers worldwide. Managers point out that specific social norms, legal guidelines, consumer lifestyles, and the external environment in which they operate determine how committed they need to be to green issues. Their products and services reflect how the immediate external environment supports their commitment to green initiatives. However, an enterprise's commitment to green initiatives depends also on the functional, physical, and psychological sophistication of its products and services. Usually the higher the technological sophistication of an enterprise, the greener the products and services it markets. Green consumers in more-advanced markets do not necessarily agree with this generalization and argue that even technologically green products contain materials that, if not properly recycled, damage the physical environment.

High-technology electronics such as energy efficient and smart hand-held devices, including computers, are considered green products in most world markets and do not involve extensive differentiation from market to market — a single version may be sold globally. Products with lower technological sophistication such as nondurable consumer goods require more product differentiation. The green image of a smaller manufacturing enterprise depends on the ethical and professional reputation of its commitment to green initiatives. Enterprises which differentiate their level of green commitment in foreign markets most likely have mixed green images from market to market. For example, a well-known global home appliance manufacturer markets washing machines which range from hand-operated models requiring large amounts of water and detergent for each cycle to solar powered models with water recirculating and filtering systems, including automatic detergent dispensing features over several cycles. It is difficult for this manufacturer to defend its green image in markets where energy and water are at a premium and hand-operated washing machines are generally used.

Consumers define green products and services in most markets by deciding which products and services are green and which are not. This is a subjective decision by consumers. Even when smaller manufacturing enterprises market products and services as green, consumers may reject them as green. Consumers in some international markets reject products and services classified as green due to local conditions. The conditions may be cultural because a new green product is not as good as the old product, social because green products are not matched with local consumption, or technological because green products are too advanced and have a steep learning curve.

It is difficult for managers of smaller manufacturing enterprises to formulate a single green marketing strategy for all market segments of international markets. They need to examine and evaluate market segments and entire foreign markets in order to develop a comprehensive portfolio designed to match their green products and services with the market segments and individual foreign markets. Each enterprise must decide to market products or services in all markets or a single product or service in a single market. This is a difficult decision according to some marketing managers among smaller manufacturing enterprises and very much dependent on the level of green commitment as constrained by financial resources.

7.2 Consumer Responses to Green Products and Services

Consumer responses to green products and services are complex. Market responses and demand fluctuations are generally received as information feedback, which may come through various information channels. Consumer responses can be received directly from consumers via communication media such as the Internet or as feedback through supply channels. The retail portion of the supply channel can provide feedback as lost sales revenue, number of returned products, unsolicited complaints, technical support issues, or other concerns and complaints. Intermediaries in the supply channel are also sources of consumer information. Any consumer feedback, regardless how it was received, needs to be collected, processed, and provided to top decisions makers.

Consumer feedback from unsolicited sources must be considered along with marketing research studies designed to collect proprietary information. Information sources need to be combined and confirmed by systematic marketing research studies and such results used to adjust marketing strategies, if not entire marketing initiatives. Managers of smaller manufacturing enterprises often consider the entire process of collecting and processing information along with marketing research studies as an investment not as an expense. Consumer information about green products or services may be positive or negative and indicates how satisfied or dissatisfied consumers are with their purchases.

Consumer satisfaction or, dissatisfaction, is typically described as the difference between what consumers expected from products and services and to what degree their expectations were met. Consumer satisfaction is a cultural matter that differs from one market to another and may be present during the actual purchase, consumption, or post-consumption. Marketing managers suggest that differentiating between positive and negative responses for green products and services is relatively predictable, but measuring or otherwise specifying levels of consumer satisfaction is more problematic.

Consumers ultimately decide how satisfied they are with green products and services and are concerned about how green products and services contribute to their individual lifestyles. Some consumers worry about how much the green products and services they consume contribute to broad social goals for energy conservation or dependency on nonrenewable resources. Thus, it is difficult to assess consumer satisfaction from the perspective of personal consumption without considering the nature of the entire consumption process — economic, social, or psychological consumption. Each consumption process generates a different level of satisfaction.

Measuring or otherwise specifying consumer satisfaction for green products and services in international markets is even more complex. Nevertheless, even simply ranked estimates of consumer satisfaction are important to marketing managers and provide valuable feedback for improving products and services, market adjustments, or other marketing actions. Observation and participatory research methods are sometimes important approaches in international markets in determining relative levels of consumer satisfaction. Marketing management driven managers of smaller manufacturing enterprises are developing methodologies to better understand consumer satisfaction across international markets. Some are based on comparative or simulation analysis. Three more conventional methodological approaches for assessing consumer satisfaction across markets are also used, sometimes sequentially or individually.

The first approach focuses on products' functional attributes. Marketing managers analyze the relationship between the intended functional product attributes identified via marketing research studies and those systematically developed by a formal new product development process. The results are compared by examining the intended uses consumers assign to a green product or service, more exactly consumers' functional expectations. If the design attributes and consumers' intended attributes match exactly, consumer satisfaction is at its maximum. The gap between design attributes and consumers' intended use attributes is a measure of the level of consumer satisfaction; most such measures are qualitative and subjective. Several objective quantitative measures can be used to determine levels of functional consumer satisfaction — tracking the number of products returned, messages received concerning functional attributes, complaints filed about functional deficiencies, or rejection of products for nonfunctionality during sales.

The second approach focuses on products' physical attributes. The physical components of green products, according to marketing managers, provide an important basis for examining levels of consumer satisfaction. A product contains materials and ingredients that constitute the whole product. If any physical attribute of a green product does not meet green consumer expectations or specifications, consumer satisfaction may be jeopardized. Consumer satisfaction is generally directly related to the appearance of a green product since the physical appearance for many consumer products is more important than the products' internal workings. Consequently, there are two indications of consumer satisfaction concerned with a product's physical attributes — product returns due to technical acceptance, failure or dissatisfaction with the physical appearance of a product. Both aspects can be quantified by collecting data and information via various information channels.

The third approach focuses on the psychological attributes of products or services and is often expressed as consumers' emotional expectations. Consumers' emotional expectation for green products and services range from clearly articulated expectations to highly subjective imaginary depictions of green products or services. However, psychological expectations are accepted as fundamental concepts of consumer behavior — perceptions, preferences, and attitudes. It is important to understand that consumers perceive needs and wants for green products and services that can be identified such as solar panels, electric automobiles, or chemically free food. Consumers also can articulate preferences for electric automobiles with a driving range over one hundred miles on a battery charge. Once consumers use products or services, they form positive or negative attitudes about them. Marketing managers of smaller green manufacturing enterprises must be able to integrate information about perceptions, preferences, and attitudes into their understanding of consumer satisfaction based on the psychological attributes of green products and services.

Market visibility and social performance are components of consumer responses to green products and services. Green consumers want to consume green products and services, be satisfied with their consumption, and also be socially visible to demonstrate that they are green. For example, owners of electric automobiles clearly feel they are conserving energy, not polluting the physical environment, and contributing to the energy awareness of others. Another example of social awareness is consumers willing to pay more for electricity every month because they support development of wind energy. Such individuals represent green consumers who, by their own consumption of green products and services, are willing to reach out to society because the products and services they consume are highly visible in the market.

7.3 Consumption Experiences of Green Consumers

Marketing managers responsible for green marketing initiatives among smaller manufacturing enterprise agree that consumers have various motivations for becoming green consumers and changing their consumption habits and lifestyles. Based on personal perceptions of what green consumption represents, there are significant numbers of consumers who aspire to become green. Other consumers justify their aspirations within their available personal finances, time constraints, or other personal constraints that do not allow them to become green and consequently postpone realization of their aspirations. Some potential green consumers collect information about their favorite green products but have minimal intention to purchase. Other consumers may be motivated to purchase a green product or service on a trial basis but subsequently reject it for various personal reasons. The major focus is on potential green consumers who will purchase a green product or service and become satisfied repeat consumers. Many of these aspirations and motivations are explained by how consumers approach purchases of products or services in terms of perceptions, preferences, and attitudes.

Consumer perceptions of green product and services serve an important role in defining markets, market segments, and developing consumer profiles. Consumer perceptions reveal how potential consumers view products and services — what they think about them and what their mental impressions are of green products and services. Consumer perceptions reflect personal cognitive and behavior factors; their perceptions differ greatly, especially across international markets, depending on cultural and socio-economic differences. An important task in examining consumer preferences is the percentage of potential consumers who anticipate purchasing a green product or service and eventually make a purchase and become satisfied consumers. Marketing managers need to constantly reinforce the anticipation and motivation of consumers who have positive perceptions of green products and services to make a purchase.

Consumer preferences for green products and services are more important for marketing managers than perceptions. Consumers who prefer green products and services generally have had positive experience with previous green purchases, consumption, and, in some cases, post-consumption. Their propensity to change consumption and lifestyles is higher than among segments of consumers who only positively perceive green products and services. Green consumers are generally perceived as innovators or early adopters of green products and services and become advocates for them.

Green consumers frequently communicate their preferences via the Internet by participating in Internet based discussions, responding to surveys, and offering testimonials. Managers of smaller manufacturing enterprises may manage green product support websites and encourage discussions about a range of issues concerning green consumption and lifestyles. By doing so, marketing managers have an opportunity to integrate green products and services in complementary or supplementary lifestyles and thereby expand their markets. Internet based support websites for green products and services suggest that availability frequently limits preferences for green products and services. In turn, lack of availability of green products and services points to further green opportunities for smaller manufacturing enterprises.

Consumption and post-consumption experiences influence the attitudes green consumers form about a product or service. After consumers try a green product or avail themselves of a green service, they form positive or negative attitudes; both are beneficial to marketing managers of smaller manufacturing enterprises. Positive attitudes reinforce green marketing initiatives, generate green demand, and form markets; they also reinforce repetitive purchases and create dedicated and long-lasting consumption of green products and services. Negative attitudes of green consumers motivate smaller manufacturing enterprise to innovate and offer better green products and services.

7.4   Consumption Patterns of Green Consumers

Marketing managers responsible for new product development among smaller manufacturing enterprises focus on consumption experiences of potential and present green consumers. Consumption experiences and more stable consumption patterns indicate how consumers integrate green products and services into their entire consumption processes and green lifestyles.

Green consumers consume green products and services on three levels — economic, social, and psychological. Each level represents different motivations, consumption patterns, and lifestyles. Green products and services may be purchased for economic reasons because consumers have limited finances but want to feel that they are contributing to green causes. More socially conscious green consumers consume green products and services intentionally because such purchases are socially visible and provide them with social status. Electric automobiles, solar panels installed on private homes, or rain gardens have high social profiles. Green consumers who have a strong need to purchase green products and services for themselves regardless of the cost of the product or social visibility consume on a psychological level. Examples are found in home construction where individuals build completely self-contained energy-efficient homes based on the latest technology.

Consumers' green experiences differ across domestic and foreign markets and must be considered within each distinct market. Smaller manufacturing enterprise managers frequently point out that some markets for green products and services are very stable when measured by demand, pricing, and consumption indicators. In economically or socially challenged economies, markets for green products and services are unstable when the same measures are used. However, regardless of market stability, green consumers tend to start with consumption of green products and services that directly impact their day-to-day needs. Most green consumers in stable markets suggest that green products and services lower the cost of living and point to such innovations as solar panels that generate enough energy for a single dwelling and create a surplus of energy that can be turned into a subsidy. Other examples point to energy-efficient home appliances, electric bicycles, electric lawn mowers, among other energy-efficient products. Marketing managers need to understand the progression of what green products and services green consumers purchase and in what sequence. Understanding the sequencing of purchases of green products and services in existing markets and projecting evolution of future markets is important for marketing managers, especially among more innovative and consumer proactive smaller manufacturing enterprises.

Consumption of green products and services creates different challenges for green consumers in economically or socially challenged markets and may provide minimal savings. This is primarily due to increased and compounded consumption opportunities. For example, the availability of inexpensive wind or solar energy in small rural villages may lead to purchases of new products and services — availability of the Internet, television viewing, personal computers, or telephones. These devices increase personal expenditures and contribute to modified lifestyles. Introduction of other green products or services in similar markets may improve health delivery, transportation options, or social green initiatives.

Understanding how green consumers sequence purchases of green products and services may be used to predict trends in social consumption. When small segments of consumers begin to consume green products and services, their consumption becomes socially visible and may change how the rest of the society judges green products or services. Acceptance of green products and services inevitably produces a chain of products that may not be socially visible but nevertheless impact environmental conditions and the lifestyles of others. Examples can be found in energy conservation and utilization of natural resources in architecture, agriculture, and healthcare, among other socially significant human activities. Construction of energy-efficient homes calls for energy-efficient construction materials, lighting, plumbing fixtures, and electrical appliances in addition to other requirements. New equipment is needed for new methods of organic farming and new energy-efficient farms may be built to house life stock. Such innovations have an impact on the immediate environment and are socially visible because of their design, physical shape, or other characteristics — lower noise levels, new landscaping patterns, or low maintenance.

Consumption of green products and services takes place on two levels — personal consumption and public consumption. Consumers decide which green products and services they want to consumers and what kind of green lifestyles they want to live. Personal consumption of green products can be socially visible and motivate other consumers. Green consumption forms the platform for public green consumption. Public green consumption consists of socially visible green products and services which project collective public benefits. Public administrators in a number of major markets are cooperating with private consumers on green initiatives. Cities build public mass transit systems and the initial designs may offer special parking for commuters on bicycles, recharging stations for electric automobiles, or pick up areas for commuters. Many of these green public initiatives are closely tied to green materials, components, or products. Cooperation between smaller green manufacturing enterprises and green public projects is growing.

Public perceptions of green products or services in the public sector are complex issues which are important in harmonizing private and public perceptions of green products and services. Conflicts between private and public use of green products or services are important in analyses of markets with differing cultures, levels of technology, and environmental conditions and must be considered when developing green products and services for a variety of international markets.

Individual perceptions concerning publicly accepted green products or services are also an issue since perceptions of public green products or services may be positive or negative. Negative perceptions are much more relevant to development and market introduction of innovative green products and services. A citizen may object to a wind turbine built close to a private residence or an individual may object to a public rain garden that attracts undesirable wildlife. Group perceptions of green products and services tend to challenge or confront beliefs, values, and acceptance of green issues important to the public. Older residents may object to development of an aesthetically unappealing old municipal building intended for conversion into energy-efficient modern apartments for a younger population. Systemic acceptance or rejection of green products or services must also be considered. An example of positive perceptions of green products or services on a systemic level is the acceptance of electric automobiles by an entire country as is the case in Norway. Rejecting natural gas or biofuels is an example of negative perceptions leading to complete rejection of green products or services.

It is important to understand how consumption of green products and services changes private and public attitudes to green initiatives. Perceptions of green consumption by individual consumers and the public are important although visible green consumption changes from market to market and country to country. Green consumption in advanced markets is increasingly more socially important and expectation of green initiatives range from marketed green products and services to the physical facilities from which smaller manufacturing enterprises market their products. The public expect green products and services to originate in green facilities as much as do green consumers. Green facilities are perceived as clean modern places and structures, powered by green energy, and utilizing the latest clean technologies. Many green consumers consider these as realities that marketing managers of smaller manufacturing enterprises must accept.

7.5   Post-Consumption and Product and Service Residuals

Post-consumption concerns are a new phenomenon among green consumers and present additional challenges for smaller manufacturing enterprises. Green consumers are concerned with post-consumption in markets where green products and services are readily available and private or public facilities operate to recycle or otherwise dispose of consumption residuals. They think of the entire consumption process as a sequence of events from the decision to purchase a product or service to the point when the product no longer has any value. Alternatively, green consumers extend their notion of green consumption past a product's or service's economic, social, or psychological life. They believe that the marketing system is responsible for product and service residuals and expect product and service residuals to be processed, recycled, or disposed of under environmentally safe conditions.

Green consumers need to maintain recycling facilities and to spend time sorting waste and other consumption residuals. They expect that systems are available for extending the value of used products or the residuals. If a green consumer no longer perceives any psychological value in a product, whatever the product may be — clothing, appliance, and furniture — the consumer may decide to sell the product on the Internet or use another social system for its disposal. Some green consumers argue that when a product is completely used — functionally, physically, or psychologically — it is the responsibility of the original source to take it back.

These arguments are not without precedent. Automobile tires are routinely recycled in most advanced markets worldwide. Batteries of all kinds must be disposed of under strict environmental conditions. However, if a product has any material value left at the end of its life cycle, it may still have some value and its decomposition provides the basis for additional value in the entire industrial process such as steel, plastic, metal, or other residuals. The challenge for smaller manufacturing enterprises is to expand their notion of consumer consumption and consider the new post-consumption issues contemplated by many green consumers.

Marketing managers of smaller manufacturing enterprises must understand that green consumers, in their responses to green consumption, believe that green consumption is a two-way process just as much as is the entire marketing effort. Consumers in more-advanced consumer-focused markets are asking for closer communication with those responsible for green products and services. Smaller green manufacturing enterprises attempt to communicate with consumers via the Internet. Every webpage has an option where consumers can leave messages and information that concerns them personally. Smaller green manufacturing enterprises maintain comprehensive databases about consumers in order to provide better services. It is becoming obvious, that in the framework of green consumption, smaller green manufacturing enterprises need to have closer and more intimate relationships with green consumers. These trends have already emerged in more-advanced markets such as in North America, the Nordic countries, and most major European countries. Similar incipient trends will follow in less matured consumer markets.

Recommended Reading

1. Hawkins, D. I. and Motherbaugh, D. (2012). *Consumer Behavior: Building Marketing Strategy*, 12th edition (McGraw-Hill/Irwin, New York, NY).

Chapter 8

International Implications of Green Strategies and Consumption Behavior

An increasing number of smaller manufacturing enterprises participate in international marketing activities. They respond to various market demands from green consumers. Each international market exhibits different levels of consumer demand for green products and services. Consumer inputs and demands for green consumer products and services are high in economically and socially advanced markets, but substantially lower in economically and socially challenged markets.

Two constantly changing aspects of international green markets challenge managers of smaller green manufacturing enterprises. The first challenge is the prevailing technology and economic and social conditions in international markets. Managers of smaller manufacturing enterprises perceive that higher technology green products and services are in demand in more-advanced green markets. Conversely, they perceive that more low-technology green products and services are purchased in less-advanced green markets. The second challenge is the expectations of green consumers and the willingness of smaller green manufacturing enterprises to fulfill them. Most managers of smaller green manufacturing enterprises consider the complex issues of the two challenges as relevant to formulating green marketing strategies and to understanding green initiatives in international markets.

8.1   International Markets and Technology

How advanced an international market for green products and services is depends on the technological sophistication of consumers in that market. More specifically, it depends on the predominant understanding consumers have of the technology available to them in their market. Technology, in most markets today, is understood as the means and ways the public accomplishes its objectives in a commonly accepted and compatible fashion. From a cultural perspective, technology is an evolutionary process that reflects how society accomplishes things collectively. Technology often evolves from social norms, habits, and customs.

High-technology products and services are available and used in advanced markets by a significant number of consumers who understand prevailing technology. Such green consumers are the innovators or early adopters of green products and services based on the latest available technology. This is important for marketing green products and services in advanced markets to well-informed green consumers. Green consumers frequently look for green products and services outside of their local markets by using telecommunication channels of communication, social media, and the Internet. They are willing to source green products and services across borders for the latest technology. Green consumer tendencies to seek the latest technology abroad increases international competition for smaller manufacturing enterprises that may not be represented in every international market. However, green consumers in any market may be able to reach a smaller manufacturing enterprise directly if the enterprise has posted a webpage. The enterprise can then decide if it will respond to the inquiry.

A number of smaller green manufacturing enterprises sell and support green products in international markets through special agents such as local representatives, importers, or sales agents. Depending on the nature of the green products, enterprises maintain technical support staff to service international green customers. Similar arrangements are offered by smaller manufacturing enterprises that provide services in international markets through a local agency.

Some enterprises provide a dedicated team of specialists to render the service. For example, an installation of solar cells in a geographically remote location may require regular maintenance from the enterprise that sold the installation. A service provider offering design and construction of weather insulated and energy-efficient recreational homes maintain a team of internationally experienced designers and construction specialists certified in several countries.

Examining green opportunities in advanced markets worldwide presents a challenge for many smaller manufacturing enterprises. The decision to market green products and services internationally may offer potentially profitable options that can be realized by understanding what motivates green consumers in advanced markets to purchase products or services from a foreign supplier. It is the technological content of the products and services that motivates green consumer demand, according to managers of smaller manufacturing enterprises experienced in green international marketing transactions.

Consumer demand for green products and services in less-advanced markets does not necessarily indicate the level of technology generally found in such markets. The established technology may vary from high to low and may reflect various market segments with differing consumption behaviors and lifestyles. The specific segment differences can be accounted for by demographics, socio-demographics, or lifestyles. The differences in consumption behavior and lifestyles also can be accounted for by technological preferences and actual use of green products and services.

According to managers of smaller green manufacturing enterprises that are extensively engaged in less-advanced markets, their market segments for technologically advanced green products and services are the educated, more affluent, and widely traveled green consumers who are aware of green high-technology products and services in other markets. Most green consumers in less-advanced markets tend to consume green products or services inconspicuously. Consumers in other segments of less-advanced markets may, intentionally or unintentionally, consume lower technology green products and services.

8.1.1   *Cultural conditions*

There are many anomalies in international markets regarding the use of technology since technology is also related to culture. A market's indigenous cultural conditions may create barriers for green products or services. For example, in some remote rural markets of the world, the elders did not openly embrace the introduction of solar energy to power laptop computers in local schools. Another example from international markets illustrates the reluctance to accept new light source options available for saving energy. The new light sources do not necessarily emit light as quickly as the old light bulbs did. Consumers in markets around the world want immediate light; they think something is wrong if the light sources do not emit light immediately.

Cultural barriers to green products and services also exist in other, relatively stable, international markets. For example, home appliances such as washing machines are increasingly more efficient in more-advanced markets and minimize destructive impact on all types of fabrics; they also use less energy, water, and detergent, in addition to better protecting the contents. These technologically advanced appliances contrast with similar appliances in less-advanced markets where hand-operated washing machines use more water, do not use detergent, and are harmful to the content. Beyond the availability of energy as the differentiating factor, the differences between the two markets can be accounted for by well-rooted cultural practices and habits. Managers of smaller green manufacturing enterprises specializing in developing green products and services for economically and socially challenged markets suggest that, even when wind- or solar-generated electricity is available to power a new generation of washing machines, the local population is reluctant to use them.

8.1.2   *Resources*

Green consumers in some international markets are concerned about the availability of resources which support their current lifestyles. The resources inherent in these markets traditionally are used to conduct their day-to-day activities. Many consumer products and services correspond closely to locally available resources. Local fuels used for cooking such as wood, coal, or other organically derived fuels contribute to air pollution. However, consumers have few alternatives due to economic and social conditions in these markets. Green consumers in these markets are trying to replace local fuels with nonpolluting substitutes such as wind, solar power, or natural gas. Replacing the cooking and heating fuel also produces demand for other green products and services designed to not deplete local resources and pollute the environment. Smaller green manufacturing enterprises must understand these conditions as opportunities for new green products and services.

Similar conditions exist in agriculture where depletion of arable soils and lack of available water for irrigation in many countries are moving farmers to modern technology-based processes such as aqua-farming, greenhouse vegetable cultivation, or water-efficient vertical farming methods. These high-technology food-producing methods are directly tied to two fundamental green approaches. First, green consumers are behind the demand for better agricultural products produced in ways that save resources, especially water. In some markets, green consumers form alliances with organic farmers to secure their supplies of fresh green products since organic farmers need specialized equipment that saves water and soil, and uses organic fertilizer, or otherwise saves resources. Relationships between organic farmers and green consumers exist in advanced and less-advanced markets, but not to the same degree. This situation offers potential for smaller manufacturing enterprises to cooper-ate with agricultural producers and market green products and services.

An equally important green approach begins directly with smaller green manufacturing enterprises. Some traditional smaller manufac-turing enterprises have initiated a transition from marketing conven-tional electronic equipment used in generating energy to small-scale compact energy generating sources. Managers of these enterprises often see these transitions as normal technological responses to market needs. For example, an enterprise manufacturing gasoline-driven stationary generators, as standby electricity generators, now produces natural gas-powered units. The enterprise also supplements its energy generating line by fabricating compact wind-powered generators suitable for supplying a large agricultural installation. For other markets, the enterprise has engineered a solar-powered installation that produces electricity, heats water, and provides a continuous power supply for small rural medical centers.

Utilization and preservation of resources are connected to cultural issues and lifestyles in many international markets that provide green opportunities and initiatives. In some markets, this is driven by green consumers or consumers who want to be green. At the same time, if marketing managers of smaller green manufacturing enterprises assess international markets in the context of marketing management, they should be able to systematically identify green opportunities and initiatives.

8.1.3 *Awareness*

Consumers in most international markets become aware of green products and services due to the ease and ability of communicating with other consumers and enterprises across markets. The Internet has become the primary platform for green consumption and life changing experiences. Green consumers can purchase green products or services in other than their home market and have them delivered in their home market by local distribution centers. In many instances, smaller manufacturing enterprises do not necessarily need proprietary distribution channels but can assign their products or services to fulfillment specialists. Most green consumers worldwide are aware of such buying options.

Awareness of green products and services ranges from high in more-advanced markets, mostly due to better quality communication options, to low in economically and socially challenged markets. Nevertheless, depending on the level of awareness, green consumers approach green products and services differently in their consumption and post-consumption experiences. They emphasize green consumption in some markets, while in other markets green consumers focus on consumption and post-consumptions. Consumers in more-advanced markets buy green products and use green services because they are committed to green lifestyles; both consumption and post-consumption are important to them. Consumers in less-advanced markets are aware of the benefits of green products and services, but often for the wrong reasons. Consumers may find the appearance of green products appealing, the protective packaging interesting because of its potential to be used for other purposes, or, in some markets, because it might be fashionable to buy green products.

International marketing managers of smaller manufacturing enterprises suggest that consumers' awareness of green products and services can lead these enterprises to green market opportunities and initiatives. For example, awareness of green products and services and their availability via the Internet frequently draws enterprises to various international markets — including more- or less-advanced markets. In addition, consumers' awareness of green products and services, more specifically their unavailability, provides an unfilled demand in the market. Some managers maintain a portfolio of international markets and decide when to enter additional markets by measuring awareness of green products and services in the most likely market segment with the greatest potential to purchase them. They also monitor imports of green products into potential markets and, when imports reach a significant demand level, they enter the markets directly.

It is important to realize that in international markets, regardless of how advanced the markets are, consumers must first become aware of green products and services before they can consume them. At some point in consuming green products and services, green consumers become concerned about what happens at the end of their life cycles. Post-consumption concerns are closely tied to green consumption for some green consumers. Green consumers in more-advanced markets are much more interested in the life cycle of green products and services than green consumers in less-advanced markets. Marketing managers of smaller manufacturing enterprises are often puzzled by the notion that consumers in economically and socially challenged markets have lower tolerances for green issues. This does not mean that the managers should lower their standards for green issues in these markets, rather it signals an opportunity for providing consumers with a better understanding of green issues.

8.2   Expectation for Green Products and Services

A complex problem for international marketing managers of smaller green manufacturing enterprises is the interaction between the expectations of green consumers about the green products and services they consume and fulfillment of their expectations by the smaller green manufacturing enterprises. These interactions between enterprises and green consumers reflect the level of commitment by smaller green manufacturing enterprises to green products and services and the levels of expectations for green products and services by consumers. Commitment to green initiatives by individual enterprises range from total commitment of the entire enterprise to fulfilling green initiatives — the highest level to an enterprise only modifying existing products or services — the lowest level. Consumers may expect full commitment from an enterprise, but only receive marginally green modified products or services. The differences between what consumers expect and what they receive as green products and services create anxieties for them — what enterprises deliver as green products and services are important.

Marketing managers of smaller green manufacturing enterprises face a dilemma that differs from one international market to another. Consumers' expectations of green products and services in each international marker are defined based on predominant market conditions and their influence on consumer behavior. If a market is dynamic with consumption choices among many products and services, consumers have higher expectations from green products and services. Consumers expect the green products and services they consume to have a higher level of commitment from the enterprises that manufactured or offered the green product or service. Furthermore, the product or service makes a significant contribution to the consumer's dedication to green consumption and lifestyle.

The opposite situation exists in international markets where expectations of green consumers are low, typically because of lack of market dynamics. In international markets where green consumers' expectations are low, enterprises may deliver products or services that are only marginally green. How green the products and services are a function of each individual enterprise's green marketing strategy. An enterprise fully committed to green initiatives will most likely have equal high fulfillment targets for all international markets, which implies that the enterprise will market the same functionally green products and services in all international markets. Some enterprises differentiate among markets with low green expectations; they deploy green marketing strategies to match the consumers' low green expectations.

When international marketing managers decide how to approach international markets, they can decide to treat all international markets equally and deliver a single version of their products or services — global products marketed in global markets. Although this strategy is profitable for well-known global enterprises, it seldom works for smaller manufacturing enterprises with limited exposure to international markets. Such enterprises are more likely to develop green marketing strategies that balance the expectations of green consumers in various markets with appropriate green marketing strategies. In some cases, a smaller manufacturing enterprise will adjust individual components of a green marketing strategy without changing product or service attributes.

Most international marketing managers agree that the idea is an optimal match between consumers' expectations for green products and services and an enterprise's fulfillment of such expectations. However, any optimal match must be considered within a specified tolerance level for both consumers and enterprises — not all green consumers will be satisfied completely with every purchase and not all enterprises will formulate exact green marketing strategies for all green consumers.

When managers consider an optimal match between consumers' expectation of green products and services and the realities of what an individual enterprise can provide, it is important to understand specific expectations in terms of product and service attributes. International marketing managers suggest that in order to optimize relationships between consumers' expectations and what their enterprises can offer, they need specific information about consumers, market segments, and market dynamics in each international market. This may be expensive for less internationally focused smaller green manufacturing enterprises. Instead of directly gathering information about market compositions and dynamics, some enterprises tend to rely on secondary information or try to observe these international markets which interest them and learn which green consumers participate in those international markets and what their expectations are for green products and services.

The best practices suggest that smaller manufacturing enterprises fully committed to green initiatives conduct comparative marketing research in order to develop accurate consumer profiles which reflect consumers' expectations regarding green products and services. Consumer profiles in international markets can offer insight into consumption processes and point to products and services marketed by competitors. Consumer profiles combined with competitive positioning in a given market enable an enterprise to develop green marketing strategies that more accurately match the green expectations of consumers.

Most smaller green manufacturing enterprises have access to data collection in international markets and are able to conduct research studies over the Internet without major expenses; thus, language, cultural, or other superficial barriers can be overcome. Questionnaires or other research documents can be translated into foreign languages by knowledgeable local individuals at local universities, community colleges, or professional language services. Research questions can be placed into comprehensive research programs, which are accessible to green consumers in any selected country. Internet-based survey programs have built-in abilities to summarize and statistically analyze the collected data to generate consumer profiles or other necessary information.

It is also possible to collect information directly from previous orders or Internet inquiries. Smaller green manufacturing enterprises often maintain records about individual orders which can provide them with information such as country of origin, reorder information, frequency of orders, forms of payment, and descriptions of the products and services purchased. Such a database can also include information about consumer complaints, returned products, or dissatisfaction with services rendered. The main advantage of such a database is the descriptive information that identifies the purchase source.

If smaller green manufacturing enterprises maintain facilities abroad such as distribution centers, warehousing operations, or technical support services, they have access to additional information on logistical issues, protective green packaging, transportation, and delivery issues among others. The international marketing managers can then fine-tune green marketing strategies to better serve international green consumers.

Operating in international markets can be a challenging experience for smaller green manufacturing enterprise, especially craftsman-managed enterprises. Many craftsman- or promoter-managed enterprises are drawn into international markets by unsolicited orders, received via the Internet, from green consumers looking for more suitable green products or services. Many unsolicited orders are rejected; those eventually filled may not necessarily fulfill all the expectations of consumers requesting the product or service. In the case of craftsman- or promoter-managed smaller green manufacturing enterprises, entering international markets becomes a learning process for the managers and an experiment for the green consumers abroad. The number of repeat orders is a measure of success of how well craftsman- or promoter-managed enterprises meet green consumers' expectation in international markets.

8.3 International Market Dynamics

For experienced smaller green manufacturing enterprises managed by rational managers, entering international markets with green products and services may simply indicate a shift in focus from a domestic to an international market orientation. For such enterprises, commitment to green initiatives opens a new portfolio of green opportunities leading to an array of domestic and international markets. Managers must select the best entry strategy to reach green consumers in order to implement full commitment to green initiatives in international markets. The choices range from market entry through intermediaries familiar with various international markets to direct entry by creating wholly owned marketing operations.

Smaller green manufacturing enterprises that, for whatever reason, decide to enter international markets indirectly have options of deploying green marketing strategies by selling green products and services locally to an international trading company, to an export merchant, to a resident foreign buyer, to an export commission house, to another local manufacturer already in an international market, or to an export management company. These international entry options involve selling green products and services directly to a local entity that represents the client enterprise in an international market. This approach carries low risk, is perceived as a local transaction, and generates almost immediate cash flow. However, the client enterprise loses control over its products and services and frequently is unable to implement its intended green marketing strategy.

Smaller green manufacturing enterprises can also enter international markets indirectly through foreign agents or distributors. Although this is a relatively risk-free process, care must be taken in selecting the right agent or distributor. This is a time-consuming process at the front end, but may turn into a mutually satisfying representative process over time. One advantage of direct market entry is that a smaller green manufacturing enterprise can control how its green marketing strategy is implemented in a market where it is represented by an agent or distributor. An international marketing manager can oversee several international markets and cooperate with agents or distributors familiar with the markets they represent. Through direct communication or training, an agent or distributor becomes responsible for implementing the green marketing strategies, identifying any potential green initiatives, and reporting back to the enterprise being represented.

Similar conditions exist when managers of a smaller green manufacturing enterprise decide to open a foreign branch that generally consists of sales and technical support for products and services.

The direct branch of an enterprise is typically responsible for all marketing activities in a given market and the branch manager is responsible for marketing initiatives, sales, and technical support. Managers of smaller green manufacturing enterprises may find it difficult to identify a suitable individual to serve in that capacity. This is primarily because a branch manager must understand all aspects of the enterprise in question, including the mission, green commitment, future green initiatives, as well as the appropriate green marketing strategies intended for the branch manager's particular market. The branch manager is responsible for the success and profitability of the market in this situation. Sufficient communication between the branch manager and the key decision maker in the enterprise is important because dynamic green enterprises look for green opportunities often found in international markets.

Another option for entering international markets is to establish an independent subsidiary. Independent subsidiaries serve a somewhat different purpose than foreign branches. Subsidiaries are legal entities located in one market with the option of operating in several other contiguous or regional markets. Subsidiaries generally have more and broader responsibilities than foreign branches; subsidiaries can manufacture green products locally or render green service subject to local laws and regulations. A subsidiary usually maintains a larger physical presence while a foreign branch can function from a rented office or distribution center. International subsidiaries require larger facilities and, consequently, are more expensive to operate, but a subsidiary may be more productive and profitable long run.

Some smaller, green, high-technology manufacturing enterprises prefer to enter international markets directly. By doing so, they can reach their international consumers directly, communicate with them via the Internet and, when necessary, maintain a physical presence in those international markets. Such enterprises may still rely on local wholesalers to keep inventory and local green retailers to market appropriate products and services to consumers. However, an increasing number of smaller green manufacturing enterprises market green products and services directly to consumers via the Internet. This requires just as much knowledge of international markets as being directly located in them, but has the advantages of controlling the green marketing effort and developing green marketing strategies from one location.

The above options for entering green international markets are directly related to how committed a smaller manufacturing enterprise is to green initiatives. Beyond the green commitment, smaller green manufacturing enterprises need to define the level of their green commitment in the context of how advanced the green markets are. A full commitment to green initiatives implies a new managerial philosophy, mission, and organizational restructuring — this is an investment intensive process.

A commitment to green initiatives means meeting consumers' green expectations, which depend on the relationship between what consumers expect from green products and services, in whatever markets they are, and the willingness of smaller green manufacturing enterprises to fulfill consumers' expectations. Managers have suggested various green marketing strategies, which range from full commitment to green initiatives in all domestic or international markets to minimal commitments in marginally green domestic or international markets. The level of commitment depends on fulfillment of consumers' expectations, and top decision makers in smaller manufacturing enterprises must not forget that green consumers drive green markets and their expectations of green products and services are high. These green consumers actively seek better and more technologically advanced green products and services in global markets and thereby create green opportunities internationally for smaller green manufacturing enterprises.

Recommended Readings

1. Gesteland, R. R. and Seyk, G. F. (2002). *Marketing Across Countries in Asia* (Copenhagen Business School Press, Copenhagen, Denmark).
2. Tesar, G. and Kuada, J. (2013). Editors, *Marketing Management and Strategy: An African Casebook* (Routledge, London, UK).

Chapter 9

Integration

The research objective was to learn how smaller manufacturing enterprises commit to green marketing strategies. The main purpose was to map all major parts of the decision process and formulate a conceptual framework to understand, from the perspective of marketing management, what managerial considerations are important in committing to green initiatives. It is difficult to construct a comprehensive all-inclusive framework due to the diversity of how smaller manufacturing enterprises are managed and operate in competitive domestic and foreign markets. Based on our research, we believe that the following framework provides at least a start in developing a more comprehensive model in the future (see Fig. 9.1).

There are two primary considerations in examining smaller manufacturing enterprises to describe how they commit to green initiatives and eventually formulate green marketing strategies. The first consideration is that consumers drive almost the entire demand for green products and services. This is apparent in more-advanced markets of Europe, North America, and Australia, among other countries but similar trends are emerging in the less-advanced markets of Africa, China, and South America. The second consideration is the level of commitment managers of smaller manufacturing enterprises make to green initiatives. Some commit completely to green initiatives, without any reservations, while others are reluctant to commit and respond gradually to consumer pressures, sometimes with minimal support from top management.

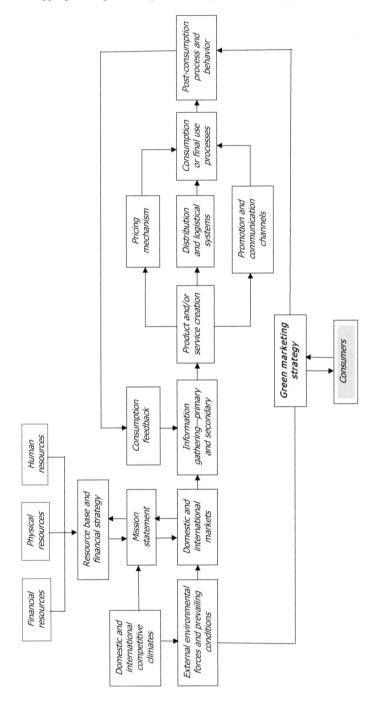

Fig. 9.1 Mapping managerial implications of green strategy: A framework for sustainable innovation.

Developing a comprehensive framework to describe managerial initiatives involved in making major decisions among smaller manufacturing enterprises requires a broad perspective and deeper assessment of individual managerial philosophies and the external environment in which smaller manufacturing enterprises operate. Some managers of smaller manufacturing enterprises underestimate the impact the external environment may have on the personal managerial philosophies and perspectives on green initiatives. High-technology, smaller manufacturing enterprises managed by rational managers take clues from the external environment in which they function. Some managers of smaller manufacturing enterprises, especially the craftsman type, often limit their interactions with the external environment and consumers and focus more on products or services.

Managers of innovative smaller manufacturing enterprises who pay close attention to consumers and external environmental forces develop flexible managerial philosophies and approaches to markets. They see green initiatives as innovations and develop green products and services accordingly. Green consumers become focal points of green marketing strategies, which supply them with innovative green products and services. High-technology startups tend to be more committed to green initiatives as opposed to well-established and locally oriented smaller manufacturing enterprises.

The following framework summarizes the managerial activities considered fundamental to making green commitments. Individual components of the framework are decision points essential for developing green marketing strategies. The framework includes numerous innovative activities that can lead to new designs and development of green products and services. The framework outlines a path for advances in green marketing activities, consumption, and final use of green products and services, and post-consumption processes and behaviors.

The framework is intended as a decision tool for managers of smaller manufacturing enterprises who commit to green consumer initiatives. When such managers commit to green initiatives, they become aware of various environmental challenges, consumption trends, and the seemingly unpredictable behavior of green consumers. This framework is formulated to help managers make appropriate decisions as they become green. The framework has three parts: (1) the enterprise and its mission, resources, markets, and the external environment, (2) the information gathering and evaluation process that is the foundation for product and service creation and leads to consumption and post-consumption, and (3) formulating comprehensive green marketing strategies and interacting with green consumers.

9.1 Framework for Sustainable Innovation

Committing to sustainability, conservation, and green initiatives for smaller manufacturing enterprises begins with their realization that major changes are taking place. The external environments in which they function produce economic and social challenges for them. Market demand for green products and services is growing, as consumers ask for green products and services. Worldwide, consumers are reexamining their consumption habits and considering post-consumption options. Green consumers insist that enterprises consider consumer preferences from broader perspectives; they propose that managers of smaller manufacturing enterprises committed to green initiatives think about them more systematically and apply more structured marketing approaches.

As a result of these developments, relationships between green consumers and marketing managers of smaller manufacturing enterprises are changing. Green consumers want to communicate directly with green enterprises; they want to use social media to voice their concerns. Some consumers want direct input into the value creation processes as well as before and after consumption experiences. In this context, green marketing strategies are the culmination of interactions between green consumers and marketing managers of smaller manufacturing enterprises. Green consumers perceive green marketing strategies more broadly than many marketing managers and expect that green marketing strategies begin in mutually shared external environments and end with consumers' post-consumption experiences. This is a new perspective for most marketing managers of smaller manufacturing enterprises.

The new approaches to consumption and post-consumption by green consumers and their expectations of green products and services are not uniform in domestic and international markets. Green consumers are more proactive in their approaches to consumption and post-consumption than marketing managers of smaller manufacturing enterprises. Green consumers want to consume green products and services and want control over the impact on their individual consumption and lifestyles; they have diverse expectations from green products and services. Many green consumers are active citizens and avid trendsetters. The trends set by green consumers are behind various green initiatives of smaller manufacturing enterprises — their assessment is critical.

9.1.1 *External environment and enterprise mission*

The commitment to green initiatives for many smaller manufacturing enterprises begins with a thorough review of their missions. The mission, or mission statement, provides the strategic direction for an enterprise, its unique focus, and flexibility for its future direction. The fundamental assumption behind every mission is that the enterprise will change, be innovative, grow with market opportunities, and face the future. The future for many smaller manufacturing enterprises is green. Consequently, commitment to future green initiatives must start by reexamining the mission statement and its future implications.

Decision makers in smaller manufacturing enterprises must be aware of external dynamics. They must understand the nature of domestic and international markets in which their products and services are marketed, and the competitive challenges; most of all, they must understand consumers' demands in all markets both domestic and foreign. Today, consumption patterns and lifestyles in international markets are similar to domestic markets and generate demand for similar products and services. Both domestic and foreign markets are integral parts of the broad external environment that challenge marketing managers of smaller manufacturing enterprises.

A significant number of smaller manufacturing enterprises consider themselves to be locally focused, but they face both domestic and international competition ranging from product by product or service by service competition to competitive challenges of proprietary knowledge and skills. Top decision makers responsible for formulating green marketing strategies must understand their competitors and the levels on which they compete. In addition, the domestic and foreign competitors challenging smaller manufacturing enterprises also influence developments around them. Competitive challenges inevitably stimulate innovation, new consumer lifestyles, and move other competitors to serve consumers more effectively and efficiently. Many green consumers expect the green marketing strategies of smaller green manufacturing enterprises to respond to external environmental forces and prevailing environmental conditions.

In reexamining its mission, an enterprise must consider the robustness of its resource base and flexibility of its resources — including its financial strengths and weaknesses, the capacity and flexibility of its physical resources, and the knowledge and skills of its personnel. Commitment to green initiatives requires an innovative combination of resources that often lead to major acquisitions, new resources, or redeployment of existing resources. In order to understand the dynamics of its resource base, an enterprise must understand the implications of its potential commitment to green initiatives, which typically leads to formulating additional, and frequently unexpected, financial strategies.

Managers who formulate financial strategies in smaller manufacturing enterprises must have a deep understanding of domestic and international markets because green products and services have global appeal and tend to be financially vulnerable. Green consumers have access to an abundance of information about green products or services via telecommunication or the Internet. They search for information and compare the value of green products and services across markets. Even smaller manufacturing enterprises with a local focus and reluctance to market their products internationally are within the reach of worldwide green consumers.

9.1.2 *Information and consumption*

Once a smaller manufacturing enterprise commits to green initiatives, the next step is to design the information gathering processes for both primary and secondary sources. Primary information is gathered by customized marketing research studies, panels and focus groups, and direct feedback from consumers, among other sources. Secondary information is obtained from published sources such as print or electronic media, publicly commissioned studies, community opinion panels, or other information freely available to anyone.

Primary and secondary information combined provide input into decisions by top decision makers and marketing specialists. Feedback from consumers about their consumption processes and lifestyles is also an important part of information gathering. If an enterprise is in a transition from marketing traditional products and services to marketing green products and services, there is usually a time delay in gathering sufficient information about green consumers. A learning period exists while marketing managers understand the nature of the information they need about green consumers. However, valuable information can be obtained through almost instantaneous feedback from green consumers.

Information gathered through primary and secondary sources, including consumption feedback, is used to define green products and services based on green attributes and requirements sought by green consumers. Managers of smaller manufacturing enterprises often suggest that a variety of qualitative and quantitative inputs are used in developing green products and services. This framework proposes that new green products and services are developed based on input from all levels of management ranging from top decision makers who specify the mission of the enterprise and focus on clearly defined consumers, information about domestic and international markets and competitive positions, and the financial potential. Consequently, innovative green products and services are developed for specific market segments consisting of green consumers that have been systematically identified via qualitative and quantitative studies.

Some smaller manufacturing enterprises that make a green commitment do not do so at the top managerial level; they develop green products and services by modifying or altering existing ones. This is often due to limited financial resources, not understanding consumer markets, or lack of information about the requirements of green consumers. Such approaches lack understanding of the strategic importance of green challenges to smaller manufacturing enterprises.

The pricing mechanism is an important component of green marketing strategy. The pricing mechanism sets and controls prices of green products and services, which must be based on a stipulated financial strategy combined with demand requirements and consumer preferences. Consumers' perceptions that green product and services cost more are frequently quoted as a factor in pricing green products and services. Green consumers often believe that they have to pay more to get quality green products and services. Managers of smaller manufacturing enterprises counter that although consumers' perceptions concerning prices of green products and services may be accurate, the higher prices are due to higher quality inputs and increased manufacturing and distribution costs.

Similar conditions regarding prices exist in the distribution and logistical systems for green products and services. The emphasis is mostly on green products since the distribution and logistical system is less relevant to rendering services. Green products generally require different packaging, warehousing conditions, transportation systems, and physical handling. Green consumers consider green products as being of higher quality that need to be distributed more carefully and safely. They also expect that any protective or shipping residuals can be returned. Managers of smaller manufacturing enterprises must consider options for green consumers to dispose of residuals left from protective packaging and shipping procedures when formulating green marketing strategies.

Some smaller manufacturing enterprises committed to green initiatives have developed separate distribution and logistical systems dedicated to green products. These systems clearly communicate the enterprise's dedication to green initiatives. Other components of green marketing strategies, especially the promotion and communication channels, can reassure green consumers about the benefits of dedicated distribution and logistical systems.

Green consumers relate distribution and logistical systems to consumption of green products, especially those purchased on the Internet; they expect delivery of green products to be safe and exact. Green consumers expect to be notified when packages are delivered to their destination and that packages are in a safe location, especially for deliveries of perishable goods. They expect deliveries on time as stipulated by the shipping source; green consumers expect to be notified if there are delays or if other shipping problems occur.

Promotion and communication channels are also components of a green marketing strategy. Promoting green products and services is a complex process for marketing managers of smaller manufacturing enterprises, particularly those with a lower commitment to green initiatives. There are multiple options for promoting green products and services including advertising, sales promotion, point of purchase promotion, or on sight demonstrations among others. Telecommunication and Internet promotions are increasingly important platforms for promoting green products and services. Green consumers expect direct benefits from their consumption of green products and services and want a direct connection with enterprises offering green products and services.

Marketing managers of more-advanced green consumer-focused smaller manufacturing enterprises have developed promotion options and strategies delivered via telecommunication capabilities and the Internet. They post various options on their webpages so green consumers can provide direct feedback or present specific suggestions or options. Green consumers' feedback is closely monitored and integrated into green marketing strategies. Green consumers also expect special incentives such as promotional coupons, notification of sales, or invitations to special events. Marketing managers frequently suggest that green consumers welcome promotion-based incentives and tend to be more loyal than other consumers.

The creation of products and services, their pricing, distribution, and promotion significantly impact the consumption and final use of green products and services. In the minds of green consumers, consuming green products and services differs from other consumption processes. Green consumers spend more time searching for a green product or service, educate themselves more about the benefits, and tend to build entire lifestyles around their consumption. Some green consumers tend to consume green products and services inconspicuously, while others advocate publicly visible green consumption. Marketing managers of smaller manufacturing enterprises must be aware of differences between the two approaches.

Final use of green products, and in some cases services, can be problematic for green consumers. They typically feel they should control green products or services over their entire life span, regardless of how they are consumed or used. Some green consumers point out that green products or services often cannot be co-mingled with conventional products or services. It is difficult for most green consumers to develop completely green lifestyle; they develop lifestyles based on a combination of green and conventional products and services. However, green consumers perceive increased consumption and use of green products and services based on emerging trends such as increased energy generation from wind power and reduced reliance on coal. Similar trends can be found in the home building industry and in the public transportation sector.

The interconnections between private consumption and use of green products and services and public use of resources are more obvious. These interconnections not only impact how green consumers structure their lifestyles but also define their consumption processes. This may be the most important reason why green consumers construct strong bonds with smaller green manufacturing enterprises. They expect these green enterprises to monitor emerging trends and provide innovative green products and services in response.

9.1.3   *Post-consumption*

Over the past few years, green consumers have introduced concerns over post-consumption processes and modified their behavior. They have redefined the usefulness of green products and reconsidered the role of services in their consumption. In their post-consumption phase, green consumers realize that even when green products are no longer useful, they have some economic value and need to be recycled or otherwise spent. Marketing managers among smaller green manufacturing enterprises need to consider at what point in its life cycle a product is consumed and what is left of it as they formulate green marketing strategies. The different levels of consumption — economic, social, and psychological — require secondary or tertiary markets. A major private and public dilemma is the construction and management such markets.

A limited number of smaller manufacturing enterprises of green products and services are responding to this dilemma and offering solutions such as buy backs, recycling options, or safe disposals. This approach works well for some consumer products but not all. Secondary markets for some products exist on the Internet, but typically do not involve the original enterprise. Future trends suggest that enterprises must take full responsibility for the residuals of green products.

9.2 Green Marketing Strategy and Green Consumers

Green marketing strategies reflect specific green products and services and must be directed to existing or potential green consumers. Today, green consumers signal their awareness of the changes around them and respond to them just as much as the marketing managers of smaller manufacturing enterprises respond by developing and marketing innovative green products and services.

The most important links in the overall green initiative process are the interactions between consumers and marketing managers representing smaller green manufacturing enterprises. Green consumers represent a new age of educated consumers used to operating within multichannel media and skilled in researching and purchasing products and services over the Internet. Marketing managers among smaller manufacturing enterprises must realize the need to be innovative in all aspects of their green marketing initiatives.

Postscript

Before we started this project, in the spring of 2014, we had many discussions about green initiatives among smaller manufacturing enterprises with colleagues at the Aalborg University International Business Centre. We then discussed commitment to green initiatives with managers of smaller manufacturing enterprises in North America. In early 2015, we surveyed approximately two thousand Danish managers about their attitudes toward green initiatives — after all, many considered Denmark as the greenest country in the world. We asked our colleagues in other EU countries about green initiatives. Because we work with doctoral students from several African countries, we discussed these issues with them as well. We learned a lot!

During our study, we discovered that many managers of smaller manufacturing enterprises were committing to green initiatives because international markets are looking for green products and services. The wind turbine industry is growing internationally and more energy is generated by wind power. Demand for installations of industrial and residential solar cells is growing at an unprecedented rate. Green products and services sold in retail stores and specialty shops are purchased by green consumers in all markets in Europe, North America, Australia, and other consumer markets. Norway leads the way in the number of electric cars sold per capita, motivated by government subsidies and an abundance of green energy from hydro dams. Sweden burns garbage to heat population centers in the North and imports garbage from Norway to reduce pollution and generate electricity. Innovative green products and services have been introduced in several African countries by young entrepreneurs looking for opportunities to start green initiatives.

Most green initiatives are continuing. Green consumers look for green products and services worldwide, and the Internet is experiencing a greater volume of searches. Smaller green manufacturing enterprises, even in remote parts of the world, receive inquiries about purchasing green products. Smaller manufacturing enterprises that render green services are experiencing increased in demand. Consumers in more-advanced markets are changing their consumption habits and lifestyles and are increasingly more concerned about post-consumption options. Smaller green manufacturing enterprises seek marketing opportunities in international markets.

What has changed over the life course of our project are the political and social forces that shape green awareness in general. Recent elections in a number of countries have led to conservative governments that are not interested in sustainability, conservation, or preservation of natural resources. Government subsidies for green products and services have been removed. Solar energy is being moved aside to make way for renovation of coal-based technology and automobile mileage standards have been reduced. In countries where conservation is no longer in fashion, consumers in general are less concerned about green products and services and look for less expensive and faster alternatives.

Managers of smaller manufacturing enterprises can now be classified into two major categories; those who care and those who do not care about green initiatives. The first category, those who care about green initiatives in their managerial philosophy, recognize the need to conserve resources, listen to green consumers, and deliver the best possible green products or services. Such smaller green manufacturing enterprises can be found all over the world; they care about their natural environment, who they are as manufacturers, and find green initiatives profitable. The second category consists of smaller manufacturing enterprises that initially made a low commitment to green initiatives and found it not interesting to renew their commitments when the political and social forces changed. They consider only those green initiatives that are potentially profitable. Although both types, in some way, contribute to sustainability, conservation, and preservation of nonrenewable resources, there are now fewer self-driven commitments or altruistic green initiatives.

Nevertheless, we consider this publication as a guidebook designed to help those managers of smaller manufacturing enterprises who, because they care, believe in sustainability, conservation, and preservation of natural resources to help them have a better managerial understanding of green initiatives and how to proceed in their green decision-making.

Additional Resources

Books

1. Anderson, R. C. (2011). *Business Lessons From a Radical Industrialist* (St Marin's Press, New York, NY), pp. 307.
2. Botsman, R. and Rogers, R. (2010). *What's Mine Is Yours: The Rise of Collaborative Consumption* (Harper Business, New York, NY).
3. Chouinard, Y. (2005). *Let My People Go Surfing: The Education of a Reluctant Businessman* (Penguin Books, London, UK), pp. 272.
4. Cramer, A. and Karabell, Z. (2010). *Sustainable Excellence: The Future of Business in a Fast-Changing World* (Rodale Books, New York, NY), pp. 282.
5. Esty, D. and Winston, A. (2006). *Green to Gold: How Smart Companies Use Environmental Strategy to Innovate, Create Value, and Build Competitive Advantage* (Yale University Press, New Haven, CT), pp. 363.
6. Hawken, P., Lovins, A. and Hunter Lovins, L. (1999). *Natural Capitalism: Creating the Next Industrial Revolution* (Little Brown and Company, New York, NY), pp. 378.
7. Hollender, J. and Breen, B. (2010). *The Responsibility Revolution: How the Next Generation of Businesses Will Win* (Jossey-Bass, San Francisco, CA).
8. McDonough, W. and Braungart, M. (2002). *Cradle to Cradle: Remaking the Way We Make Things* (North Point Press, a division of Farrar, Straus, and Giroux, New York, NY), pp. 186.
9. Schumacher, E. F. (1973). *Small is Beautiful: Economics as if People Mattered* (Harper & Row, New York, NY), pp. 290.
10. Werbach, A. (2009). *Strategy for Sustainability: A Business Manifesto* (Harvard Business Press, Boston, MA), pp. 227.

175

Refereed Journals

1. Aguilera-Caracuel, J., Hurtado-Torres, N. E. and Aragón-Correa, J. A. (2012). "Does International Experience Help Firms to be Green? A Knowledge-based View of How International Experience and Organizational Learning Influence Proactive Environmental Strategies." *International Business Review* 21/5, 847–861.

2. Aguilera-Caracuel, J., Hurtado-Torres, N. E. Aragón-Correa, J. A. and Dela Torre-Ruiz, J. M. (2010). "Why Do Firms Become Green? The Influence of Internationalization on the Environmental Strategy." Paper presented at the annual meeting of the Academy of Management. August 6–10.

3. Albino, V., Balice, A. and Dangelico, R. M. (2009). "A Review of the Literature on Environmental Strategies and Green Product Development: An Overview on Sustainability-Driven Companies." *Business Strategy and the Environment* 18/2, 83–96.

4. Ambec, S. and Lanoie, P. (2008). "Does it Pay to be Green? A Systematic Overview." *Academy of Management* 22/4, 45–62.

5. Anderson, P. H., Mathews, J. A. and Rask, M. (2009). "Integrating Private Transport Into Renewable Energy Policy: The Strategy of Creating Intelligent Recharging Grids for Electrical Vehicles." *Energy Policy* 37/7, 2481–2486.

6. Ángel del Brío, J. and Junquera, B. (2003). "A Review of the Literature on Environmental Innovation Management in SMEs: Implications for Public Policies." *Technovation* 23/12, 939–948.

7. Antonietti, R. and Marzucchi, M. (2014). "Green Tangible Investment Strategies and Export Performance: A Firm-Level Investigation." *Ecological Economics* 108, 150–161.

8. Arnold, M. G. and Hockerts, K. (2011). "The Greening Dutchman: Philips' Process of Green Flagging to Drive Sustainable Innovation." *Business Strategy and the Environment* 20/6, 394–407.

9. Azzone, G. and Noci, G. (1998). "Seeing Ecology and 'Green' Innovations as a Source of Change." *Journal of Organizational Change Management* 11/2, 94–111.

10. Barbier, Edward B. (2015). "Are There Limits to Green Growth?" *World Economics* 16/3, 163–192.

11. Bansal, P. and Roth, K. (2000). "Why Firms Go Green: A Model of Ecological Responsiveness." *Academy of Management Journal* 43/4, 717–736.

12. Banerjee, S. B. (2002). "Corporate Environmentalism: The Construct and Its Measurement." *Journal of Business Research* 55/3, 177–191.

13. Banerjee, S. B. (2001). "Managerial Perceptions of Corporate Environmentalism: Interpretations from Industry and Strategic Implications for Organizations." *Journal of Management Studies* 38/4, 489–513.

14. Baumann, H., Boons, F. and Bragd, A. (2002). "Mapping the Green Product Development Field: Engineering, Policy and Business Perspectives." *Journal of Cleaner Production* 10/5, 409–425.

15. Berry, M. A. and Rondinelli, D. A. (1998). "Proactive Corporate Environmental Management: A New Industrial Revolution." *The Academy of Management Executive* 12/2, 38–50.

16. Bianchi, R. and Noci, G. (1998). "'Greening' SMEs' Competitiveness?." *Small Business Economics* 11/3, 269–281.

17. Bonini, S. and Swartz, S. (2014). "Profits with Purpose: How Organizing for Sustainability can Benefit the Bottom Line." *McKinsey on Sustainability & Resource Productivity* 2, 5–15.

18. Brammer, S. and Millington, A. (2008). "Does it Pay to be Different? An Analysis of the Relationship between Corporate Social and Financial Performance." *Strategic Management Journal* 29/12, 1325–1343.

19. Carroll, A. B. (1999). "Corporate Social Responsibility: Evolution of a Definitional Construct." *Business & Society* 38/3, 268–295.

20. Christmann, P. (2000). "Effects of 'Best Practices' of Environmental Management on Cost Advantage: The Role of Complementary Asset Management." *Academy of Management Journal* 43/4, 663–680.

21. Clemens, B. (2006). "Economic Incentives and Small Firms: Does it Pay to be Green?" *Journal of Business Research* 59/4, 492–500.

22. Clemens B. and Douglas, T. J. (2006). "Does Coercion Drive Firms to Adopt 'Voluntary' Green Incentives? Relationships among Coercion, Superior Firm Resources, and Voluntary Green Initiatives." *Journal of Business Research* 59/4, 483–491.

23. Cordano, M., Scott, M. R. and Silverman, M. (2009). "How do Small and Medium Enterprises Go 'Green'? A Study of Environmental Management Programs in the U. S. Wine Industry." *Journal of Business Ethics* 92/3, 463–478.

24. Cordeiro, J. and Sarkis, J. (2001). "An Empirical Evaluation of Environmental Efficiencies and Firm Performance: Pollution Prevention Versus End-of-Pipe Practice." *European Journal of Operational Research* 135/1, 102–113.

25. Cramer, J. (1998). "Environmental Management: From 'Fit' to 'Stretch.'" *Business Strategy and the Environment* 7/3, 162–172.

26. Cronin, J. J., Smith, J. S., Gleim, M. R., Ramirez, E. and Martinez, J. D. (2011). "Green Marketing Strategies: An Examination of Stakeholders and the Opportunities they Present." *Journal of the Academy of Marketing Science* 39, 158–174.

27. Cruz, L. B. and Avila Pedrozo, E. (2009). "Corporate Social Responsibility and Green Management: Relation Between Headquarters and Subsidiary in Multinational Corporations." *Management Decision* 47/7, 1174–1199.

28. Daily, B. F. and Huang, S. (2001). "Achieving Sustainability through Attention to Human Resource Factors in Environmental Management." *International Journal of Operations & Production Management* 21/12, 1539–1552.

29. Dangelico, R. M. and Pujari, D. (2010). "Mainstream Green Product Innovation: Why and How Companies Integrate Environmental Sustainability." *Journal of Business Ethics* 95/3, 471–486.

30. Darnall, N., Henriques, I. and Sadorsky, P. (2010). "Adopting Proactive Environmental Strategy: The Influence of Stakeholders and Firm Size." *Journal of Management Studies* 47/6, 1072–1094.

31. Darnall, N., Rigling Gallagher, D., Andrews, R. N. L. and Amaral, D. (2000). "Environmental Management Systems: Opportunities for Improved Environmental and Business Strategy." *Environmental Quality Management* 9/3, 1–9.

32. Davidson, W. N. III and Worrell, D. W. (2001). "Regulatory Pressure and Environmental Management Infrastructure and Practices." *Business Society* 40/3, 315–342.

33. Eyraud, L. and Clements, B. (2012). "Going Green." *Finance & Development* 49/2, 34–37.

34. Eweje, G. (2011). "A Shift in Corporate Practice? Facilitating Sustainability Strategy in Companies." *Corporate Social Responsibility and Environmental Management* 18/3, 125–136.

35. Fraj, E., Martinez, E. and Matute, J. (2011). "Green Marketing Strategy and the Firm's Performance: The Modeling Role of Environmental Culture." *Journal of Strategic Marketing* 19/4, 339–355.

36. Fuentes, C. (2014). "Managing Green Complexities: Consumers' Strategies and Techniques for Greener Shopping." *International Journal of Consumer Studies* 38/5, 485–492.

37. Garzella, S. and Fiorentino, R. (2014). "An Integrated Framework to Support the Process of Green Management Adoption." *Business Process Management Journal* 20/1, 68–89.

38. Gerstlberger, W., Knudsen, M. P. and Stampe, I. (2014). "Sustainable Development Strategies for Product Innovation and Energy Efficiency." *Business Strategy and the Environment* 23/2, 131–144.

39. Gilley, K. M., Worrell, D. L., Davidson III, W. N. and El-Jelly, A. (2000). "Corporate Environmental Initiatives and Anticipated Firm Performance: The Differential Effects of Process-Driven Versus Product-Driven Greening Initiatives." *Journal of Management* 26/6, 1199–1216.

40. Ginsberg, J. M. (2004). "Choosing the Right Marketing Strategy." *Sloan Management Review* 46/1, 79–84.

41. González, P., Sarkis, J. and Adenso-Díaz, B. (2008). "Environmental Management System Certification and Its Influence on Corporate Practices: Evidence from the Automotive Industry." *International Journal of Operations & Production Management* 28/11, 1021–1041.

42. Gonsález-Benito, J. and Gonsález-Benito, O. (2006). "A Review of Determinant Factors of Environmental Proactivity." *Business Strategy and the Environment* 15/2, 87–102.

43. Gonsález-Benito, J. and Gonsález-Benito, O. (2005). "A Study of the Motivations for the Environmental Transformation of Companies," *Industrial Marketing Management* 34/5, 462–475.

44. Gupta, M. C. (1995). "Environmental Management and Its Impact on the Operations Function." *International Journal of Operations & Production Management* 15/8, 34–51.

45. Gurău, C. and Ranchhod, A. (2005). "International Green Marketing: A Comparative Study of British and Romanian Firms." *International Marketing Review* 22/5, 547–561.

46. Hart, S. L. and Ahuja, G. (1996). "Does it Pay to be Green? An Empirical Examination of the Relationship between Emission Reduction and Firm Performance." *Business Strategy and the Environment* 5/1, 30–37.

47. Hass, J. L. (1996). "Environmental, ('Green') Management Typologies: An Evaluation, Operationalization and Empirical Development." *Business Strategy and the Environment* 5/2, 59–68.

48. Huang, Y. and Yen-Chun, J. W. (2010). "The Effects of Organizational Factors on Green New Product Success? Evidence from High-tech Industries in Taiwan." *Management Decision* 48/10, 1539–1567.

49. Jurik, N. C. and Bodine, R. (2014). "Social Responsibility and Altruism in Small- and Medium-Sized Innovative Businesses." *Journal of Sociology & Social Welfare* 41/4, 113–141.

50. King, A. and Lenox, M. (2002). "Exploring the Locus of Profitable Pollution Reduction." *Management Science* 48/2, 289–299.

51. Klassen, R. D. and McLaughlin, C. P. (1996). "The Impact of Environmental Management on Firm Performance." *Management Science* 42/8, 1199–1214.

52. Koch Sebastian Günther and Reinhard Michael Meck (2014). "Internationalization of Renewable Energy Companies: In Search of Gestalts." *International Business Research* 7/3, 34–58.

53. Lee, K. (2009). "Why and How to Adopt Green Management into Business Organizations? The Case Study of Korean SMEs in Manufacturing Industry." *Management Decision* 47/7, 1101–1121.

54. Leonidou, L. C., Constantine S. Katsikeas, Thomas A. Fotiadis and Paul Christodoulides (2013). "Antecedents and Consequences of an Eco-Friendly Export Marketing Strategy: The Moderating Role of Foreign Public Concern and Competitive Intensity." *Journal of International Marketing* 21/3, 22–46.

55. Lepoutre, J. and Heene, A. (2006). "Investigating the Impact of Firm Size on Small Business Social Responsibility: A Critical Review." *Journal of Business Ethics* 67/3, 257–273.

56. Lin, C. and Ho, Y. (2010). "The Influence of Environmental Uncertainty on Corporate Green Behavior: An Empirical Study with Small and Medium-Size Enterprises." *Social Behavior and Personality* 38/5, 691–696.

57. Link, S., and Eitan, N. (2006). "Standardization and Discretion: Does the Environmental Standard ISO 14001 Lead to Performance Benefits?" *IEEE Transactions on Engineering Management* 53/4, 508–519.

58. Maignan, I. (2001). "Consumers' Perceptions of Corporate Social Responsibilities: A Cross-Cultural Comparison." *Journal of Business Ethics* 30/1, 57–72.

59. Marcus, A. and Fermeth A. R. (2009). "Green Management Matters Regardless." *Academy of Management Perspectives* 23/3, 17–25.

60. Martin-Tapia, I., Aragon-Correa, J. A. and Senise-Barrio, M. E. (2008). "Being Green and Export Intensity of SMEs: The Modeling Influence of Perceived Uncertainty." *Ecological Economics* 68/1–2, 56–67.

61. Martinez, F. (2014). "Corporate Strategy and the Environment: Towards a Four-dimensional Compatibility Model for Fostering Green Management Decisions." *Corporate Governance* 14/5, 607–636.

62. Maxwell, J., Rothenberg, S., Briscoe, F. and Marcus, A. (1997). "Green Schemes: Corporate Environmental Strategies and Their Implication." *California Management Review* 39/3, 118–134.

63. McDaniel, S. W. and Rylander, D. H. (1993). "Strategic Green Marketing." *The Journal of Consumer Marketing* 10/3, 4–10.

64. Melnyk, S., Sroufe, R. and Calantone, R. (2003). "Assessing the Impact of Environmental Management Systems on Corporate and

Environmental Performance." *Journal of Operations Management* 21/3, 329–351.

65. Menon, A. and Menon, A. (1997). "Enviropreneurial Marketing Strategy: The Emergence of Corporate Environmentalism as Market Strategy." *Journal of Marketing* 61/1, 51–67.

66. Miles, M. and Covin, J. (2000). "Environmental Marketing: A Source of Reputational, Competitive, and Financial Advantage." *Journal of Business Ethics* 23/3, 299–311.

67. Min, H. and Galle, W. P. (2001). "Green Purchasing Practices of US Firms." *International Journal of Operations & Production Management* 21/9, 1222–1238.

68. Mitchell, A. and Dupre, K. (1994) "The Environmental Movement: A Status Report and Implications for Pricing." *S.A.M. Advanced Management Journal* 59/2, 35–40.

69. Molina-Azorin, J. F., Claver-Cortés E., López-Gamero, M. D. and Tarí, J. J. (2009). "Green Management and Financial Performance: A Literature Review." *Management Decisions* 47/7, 1080–1100.

70. Noci, G. and Verganti, R. (1999). "Managing 'Green' Product innovation in Small Firms." *R&D Management* 29/1, 3–15.

71. Nyquist, S. (2003). "The Legislation of Environmental Disclosures in Three Nordic Countries: A Comparison." *Business Strategy and the Environment* 12/1, 12–25.

72. Olson, E. (2008). "Creating an Enterprise-level 'green' Strategy." *Journal of Business Strategy* 29/2, 22–30.

73. Orlitzky, M. and Waldman, D. (2011). "Strategic Corporate Social Responsibility and Environmental Sustainability." *Business & Society* 50/1, 6–27.

74. Papadas, K. K. and Avlonitis, G. J. (2014). "The 4 Cs of Environmental Business: Introducing a New Conceptual Framework." *Social Business* 4/4, 345–360.

75. Paulraj, A. (2009). "Environmental Motivations: A Classification Scheme and its Impact on Environmental Strategies and Practices." *Business Strategy and the Environment* 18/7, 453–468.

76. Peattie, K. and Charter, M. (2003). "Green Marketing." in *The Marketing Book*, M. J. Baker (ed.). (An imprint of Elsevier Science, Butterworth-Heinemann), pp. 726–755.

77. Polonsky, M. (1995). "A Stakeholder Theory Approach to Designing Environmental Marketing Strategy." *The Journal of Business & Industrial Marketing* 10/3, 29–46.

78. Rahbek, E. and Neergaard, P. (2005). "Caveat Emptor — Let the Buyer Beware! Environmental Labelling and the Limitations of

'Green' Consumerism." *Business Strategy and the Environment* 15/1, 15–29.

79. Remmen, A. (2001). "Greening of Danish Industry — Changes in Concepts and Policies." *Technology Analysis & Strategic Management* 13/1 53–69.

80. Rettie, R., Burchell, K. and Riley, D. (2012). "Normalising Green Behaviours: A New Approach to Sustainability Marketing." *Journal of Marketing Management* 28/3–4, 420–444.

81. Rugman, A. M. and Verbeke, A. (1998). "Corporate Strategy and International Environmental Policy." *Journal of International Business Studies* 29/4, 819–834.

82. Russo, M. V. and Fouts, P. A. (1997). "A Resource-based Perspective on Corporate Environmental Performance and Profitability." *Academy of Management Journal* 40/3, 534–559.

83. Saha, M. and Darnton, G. (2005). "Green Companies or Companies: Are Companies Really Green, or Are They Pretending to Be?" *Business and Society Review* 110/2, 117–157.

84. Sarkis, J. (1998). "Theory and Methodology: Evaluating Environmentally Conscious Business Practices." *European Journal of Operation Research* 107/1, 159–174.

85. Schaper, M. (2002). "Small Firms and Environmental Management: Predictor of Green Purchasing in Western Australian Pharmacies." *International Small Business Journal* 20/3, 235–251.

86. Schiederig, T., Tietze, F. and Herstatt, C. (2012). "Green Innovation in Technology and Innovation Management — An Exploratory Literature Review." *R&D Management* 42/2, 180–192.

87. Sen, S. and Bhattacharya, C. B. (2001). "Does Doing Good Always Lead to Doing Better? Consumer Reactions to Corporate Social Responsibility." *Journal of Marketing Research* 38/2, 225–243.

88. Sharma, S. (2000). "Managerial Interpretations and Organizational Context as Predictors of Corporate Choice of Environmental Strategy." *Academy of Management Journal* 43/4, 681–697.

89. Sharma, S. (1998). "Proactive Corporate Environmental Strategy and the Development of Competitively Valuable Organizational Capabilities." *Strategic Management Journal* 19/8, 729–753.

90. Shrivastava, P. (1995). "Environmental Technologies and Competitive Advantage." *Strategic Management Journal* 16/S1, 183–200.

91. Shortt, K. (2012). "Does 'Going Green' Make Economic Sense?" The Leonard N. Stern School of Business Glucksman Institute for Research in Securities Markets.

92. Siegel, D. S. (2009). "Green Management Matters Only If it Yields More Green: An Economic/Strategy Perspective." *Academy of Management Perspectives* 23/3, 5–16.

93. Sweeney, Sean (2015). "Green Capitalism Won't Work." *New Labor Forum* 24/2, 12–7.

94. Taken Smith, K. and Brower, T. R. (2012). "Longitudinal Study of Green Marketing Strategies that Influence Millennials." *Journal of Strategic Marketing* 20/6, 535–51.

95. Thøgersen, J. (2006). "Media Attention and the Market for 'Green' Consumer Products." *Business Strategy and the Environment* 15/3, 145–156.

96. Tran, B. (2009). "Green Management: The Reality of Being Green Business." *Journal of Economics, Finance and Administrative Science* 14/27, 21–45.

97. Tsoutsoura, M. (2004). "Corporate Social Responsibility and Financial Performance." *Strategic Management Journal* 22/2, 125–139.

98. Vaccaro, A. and Patiño Echeverri, D. (2010). "Corporate Transparency and Green Management." *Journal of Business Ethics* 95/3, 487–506.

99. Vasi, I. B. (2006). "Organizational Environments, Framing Processes, and the Diffusion of the Program to Address Global Climate Changes among Local Governments in the United States." *Sociological Forum* 21/3, 439–456.

100. Wilcox, W. E., Wilcox, M. V. and Jares, T. (2014). "Does Being Green Result in Improved Financial Performance?" *Journal of Business and Behavioral Sciences* 26/1, 155–167.

101. Windsor, S. (2011). "Understanding Green." *The Journal for Quality & Participation* 33/4, 26–29.

102. Zhu, Q. and Sarkis, J. (2004). "Relationships Between Operational Practices and Performance Among Early Adopters of Green Supply Chain Management Practices in Chinese Manufacturing Enterprises." *Journal of Operations Management* 22/3, 265–289.

103. Zsidisin, G. A. and Siferd, S. P. (2001). "Environmental Purchasing: A Framework for Theory Development." *European Journal of Purchasing & Supply Management* 7/1, 61–73.

Webpages

1. Accenture
   Available at: www.accenture.com.
   Accessed on 6/25/2017.

2. Ceres
   Available at: https://www.ceres.org/resources/tools/sec-sustainabili
   ty-disclosure-search-tool?gclid=CLyTwqzIpdQCFYQ9gQodqjsFZg.
   Accessed on 6/5/2017.

3. Deloitte
   Available at: https://www2.deloitte.com/us/en/footerlinks/contact-
   us.html?icid=bottom_contact-us.
   Accessed on 4/25/2017.

4. Denmark
   Available at: http://denmark.dk/en/green-living/strategies-and-poli
   cies/.
   Accessed on 3/9/2017.

5. Enterprise
   Available at: http://www.enterprisecommunity.org/solutions-and-inn
   ovation/green-communities.
   Accessed on 6/23/2017.

6. EnviroLink Network
   Available at: http://envirolink.org/categories.html?do=shownews/.
   Accessed on 2/21/2017.

7. Enviro Sweden
   Available at: http://www.envirosweden.se/start/.
   Accessed on 6/14/2017.

8. European Environmental Bureau
   Available at: http://eeb.org/.
   Accessed on 11/23/2016.

9. Green Biz
   Available at: https://www.greenbiz.com/microsite/state-green-busine
   ss/state-green-business-report.
   Accessed on 10/18/2016.

10. Goteborg, Sweden
    Available at: http://www.greengothenburg.se/companies/.
    Accessed on 2/8/2017.

11. Green Business
    Available at: http://futureofbusiness.info/.
    Accessed on 1/17/2017.

12. Green Business Network
    Available at: http://www.greenbusinessnetwork.org/about/whats-a-
    green-business/.
    Accessed on 2/3/2017.

13. Greendex
   Available at: http://environment.nationalgeographic.com/environ
   ment/greendex/.
   Accessed on 7/18/2016.

14. Green Furniture Concept Sweden
   Available at: http://greenfc.com/.
   Accessed on 6/25/2017.

15. Green Impact
   Available at: https://greenimpactcampaign.org/?gclid=CLy3pd_IpdQ
   CFYE7gQodUqkNpQ.
   Accessed on 5/16/2017.

16. Green Manufacturing and Maintenance
   Available at: https://www.serdp-estcp.org/Featured-Initiatives/Green
   -Manufacturing-and-Maintenance.
   Accessed on 11/23/2017.

17. Green Technica
   Available at: https://cleantechnica.com/2012/04/15/green-manufactu
   ring/.
   Accessed on 11/23/2016.

18. Ireland Environmental Protection Agency
   Available at: http://www.epa.ie/about/qcs/.
   Accessed on 4/27/2017.

19. International Labor Organization
   Available at: http://www.ilo.org/global/topics/green-jobs/areas-of-
   work/WCMS_461943/lang--en/index.htm.
   Accessed on 5/12/2017.

20. L.E.K.
   Available at: http://www.lek.com/contact-us.
   Accessed on 6/25/2017.

21. Manufacturing with Heath
   Available at: http://www.manufacturingwithheart.com/?gclid=CJ3m
   oP7LpdQCFYEZgQod26kNtg.
   Accessed on 5/6/2017.

22. McKinsey & Company
   Available at: http://www.mckinsey.com/.
   Accessed on 6/25/2017.

23. MyEnvironment
   Available at: https://www3.epa.gov/enviro/myenviro/.
   Accessed on 6/23/2017.

24. National Environmental Policy Act
    Available at: https://www.epa.gov/nepa.
    Accessed on 6/24/2017.

25. PharmTech
    Available at: http://www.pharmtech.com/contact-pharmtech.
    Accessed on 5/20/2017.

26. Pickwick Manufacturing Services
    Available at: http://pickwick.com/.
    Accessed on 6/25/2017.

27. Product Quickstart
    Available at: http://www.productquickstart.com/?gclid=CIeptuXDpd
    QCFYE7gQodUqkNpQ.
    Accessed on 6/25/2017.

28. ScienceDaily
    Available at: https://www.sciencedaily.com/news/earth_climate/envir
    onmental_policy/.
    Accessed on 6/21/2017.

29. Skanska
    Available at: http://group.skanska.com/sustainability/green/policy-
    and-strategies-on-green/.
    Accessed on 6/23/2017.

30. Small Business Administration
    Available at: https://www.sba.gov/managing-business/running-busin
    ess/green-business-guide.
    Accessed on 6/25/2017.

31. State of Green Denmark
    Available at: https://stateofgreen.com/en.
    Accessed on 2/4/2017.

32. SustainableBusiness.com
    Available at: http://www.sustainablebusiness.com/.
    Accessed on 10/20/2016.

33. Sustainability Disclosure Database
    Available at: http://database.globalreporting.org/search/.
    Accessed on 3/21/2017.

34. The Boston Consulting Group
    Available at: https://www.bcg.com/.
    Accessed on 4/15/2017.

35. The National Academies Press
    Available at: https://www.nap.edu/read/6062/chapter/43.
    Accessed on 5/24/2017.

36. The World Bank
    Available at: http://www.worldbank.org/.
    Accessed on 2/27/2017.

37. USA.gov
    Available at: https://www.usa.gov/green.
    Accessed on 5/142017.

38. U.S. Department of Defense Environmental Research Program
    Available at: https://www.serdp-estcp.org/Featured-Initiatives/Gre
    en-Manufacturing-and-Maintenance.
    Accessed on 8/24/2016.

39. U.S. Small Business Administration
    Available at: https://www.sba.gov/managing-business/business-gui
    des-industry/manufacturing.
    Accessed on 2/11/2017.

40. Village Enterprise
    Available at: http://villageenterprise.org/?gclid=CIy588DCpdQCFYg
    lgQoduN8OEQ.
    Accessed on 4/16/2017.

Index